Oxford International Resources

4

Maths
Student Book

Tony Cotton

Caroline Clissold

Linda Glithro

Cherri Moseley

Janet Rees

Language consultants:
John McMahon
Liz McMahon

OXFORD
UNIVERSITY PRESS

OXFORD
UNIVERSITY PRESS

Great Clarendon Street, Oxford, OX2 6DP, United Kingdom

Oxford University Press is a department of the University of Oxford. It furthers the University's objective of excellence in research, scholarship, and education by publishing worldwide. Oxford is a registered trade mark of Oxford University Press in the UK and in certain other countries.

British Library Cataloguing in Publication Data

Data available

ISBN 9781382006699

9 10 8

Paper used in the production of this book is a natural, recyclable product made from wood grown in sustainable forests. The manufacturing process conforms to the environmental regulations of the country of origin.

Printed in India by Manipal Technologies Limited

Acknowledgements

The publisher and authors would like to thank the following for permission to use photographs and other copyright material:

Cover artwork by Peskimo. **Photos: p6(t):** dominique landau/Shutterstock; **p6(bl):** Typhoonski/Dreamstime; **p6(br):** dmitro2009/Shutterstock; **p17:** nanka/Shutterstock; **p19(t):** Richmatts/iStockphoto; **p19(b):** John Warburton-Lee Photography/Alamy Stock Photo; **p32(a), p35(a):** clickit/Shutterstock; **p32(b), p35(b):** Berezovskaya/Shutterstock; **p32(c), p35(c):** Volodymyr Burdiak/Shutterstock; **p32(d), p35(d):** neelsky/Shutterstock; **p32(e), p35(e):** David Havel/Shutterstock; **p37:** Pitinan Piyavatin/Alamy Stock Photo; **p38:** Chaowalit Seeneha/Shutterstock; **p52(t):** Lemberg Vector studio/Shutterstock; **p52(b):** Eichiku/Shutterstock; **p57:** Guru 3D/Shutterstock; **p62(a):** Krakenimages.com/Shutterstock; **p62(b):** Eric Isselee/Shutterstock; **p62(c):** Eric Isselee/Shutterstock; **p62(d):** Ekipaj/Shutterstock; **p62(e):** Eric Isselee/Shutterstock; **p62(f):** Jaroslava V/Shutterstock; **p65:** romawka/Shutterstock; **p66:** Stephen Whybrow/Shutterstock; **p68(ml):** tulla/iStockphoto; **p68(tr):** Ryan Mackay/Dreamstime; **p68(br):** Merydolla/Shutterstock; **p68(bl):** Rawpixel.com/Shutterstock; **p84(mr):** Nataliia K/Shutterstock; **p84(br):** Andrey_Popov/Shutterstock; **p100:** Vladimir Wrangel/Shutterstock; **p104(t):** DarioZg/Shutterstock; **p104(bl):** Iakov Filimonov/Shutterstock; **p104(br):** JUAN HERBERT GIRSANG/Shutterstock; **p121:** Duncan Cuthbertson/Shutterstock; **p128:** Ahturner/Shutterstock; **p130:** Panoramic Images/Alamy Stock Photo; **p144:** Independent Photo Agency Srl/Alamy Stock Photo; **p156(l):** G2019/Shutterstock; **p156(m):** KazT/Shutterstock; **p156(r):** Astor57/Shutterstock; **p161(l):** Vereshchagin Dmitry/Shutterstock; **p161(m):** XiXinXing/Shutterstock; **p161(r):** Konstantin L/Shutterstock; **p162:** © Lefevre Fine Art Ltd., London/Bridgeman Images; **p175(tl):** Angela Royle/Shutterstock; **p175(tm):** Vladeep/Shutterstock; **p175(tr):** ColorMaker/Shutterstock; **p175(bl):** Peyker/Shutterstock; **p175(bm):** Sharon Spiteri/Shutterstock; **p175(br):** Elena_RK/Shutterstock.

Artwork by John Batten, Q2A Media Services Pvt. Ltd and OKS.

Every effort has been made to contact copyright holders of material reproduced in this book. Any omissions will be rectified in subsequent printings if notice is given to the publisher.

The manufacturer's authorised representative in the EU for product safety is Oxford University Press España S.A. of el Parque Empresarial San Fernando de Henares, Avenida de Castilla, 2 – 28830 Madrid (www.oup.es/en).

Contents

How to use this book

The Student Book for *Oxford International Primary Maths* forms part of your mathematics lessons for this year. Your teacher will introduce the ideas through whole-class activities, then you will explore them in more depth using this book, before all coming back together to discuss what you have learned. Find out more at: www.oxfordprimary.com/international-maths

Structure of the book

This book is divided into 10 units. Each unit covers a different strand of mathematics.

What you will find in each unit

There are five types of lessons:

Engage introduces the unit's mathematical ideas.
It tells you what you will learn in the unit and includes the big question.

Discover introduces mathematical skills and concepts.

In **Explore** you practise the skills you learned in Discover.

Connect helps you make links between the different areas of mathematics in the unit.

In **Review** you show your teacher what you have learned in the unit.

What you will find in the lessons

Although each lesson is unique, they have common features:

Discover / **Explore** The lesson type tells you whether you are discovering new mathematical concepts or exploring concepts you have already been introduced to.

Key words
- value
- round

This box gives the key words for the lesson.

Stretch zone This challenges you to take your learning further.

In the speech bubbles, you will find useful hints, examples of how to complete a question, or extra questions to get you thinking about the mathematics you are doing.

Additional features

This shows you where you can practise the key vocabulary, either by writing the words or through a discussion.

This shows you where you can practise your mental maths skills such as your times tables or other key number facts.

This shows you where you need to record your work in a notebook.

Glossary Key words are listed in a picture glossary at the end of the book. You can write your own definition for each word.

Teacher's Guides

The Teacher's Guide that accompanies this book provides lesson notes for each page.

Practice Book

At the bottom of each page in this book, there is a link to the Practice Book, where you can find extra practice to do in your lesson or at home.

1 Number and place value

? How can I use my knowledge of counting to 100 to order and compare numbers greater than 1000?

In this unit you will:

- count in multiples of 6, 7, 9, 25 and 1000
- count back through zero to include negative numbers
- order and compare numbers beyond 1000
- estimate numbers using number lines
- round any number to the nearest 10, 100 or 1000.

Engage

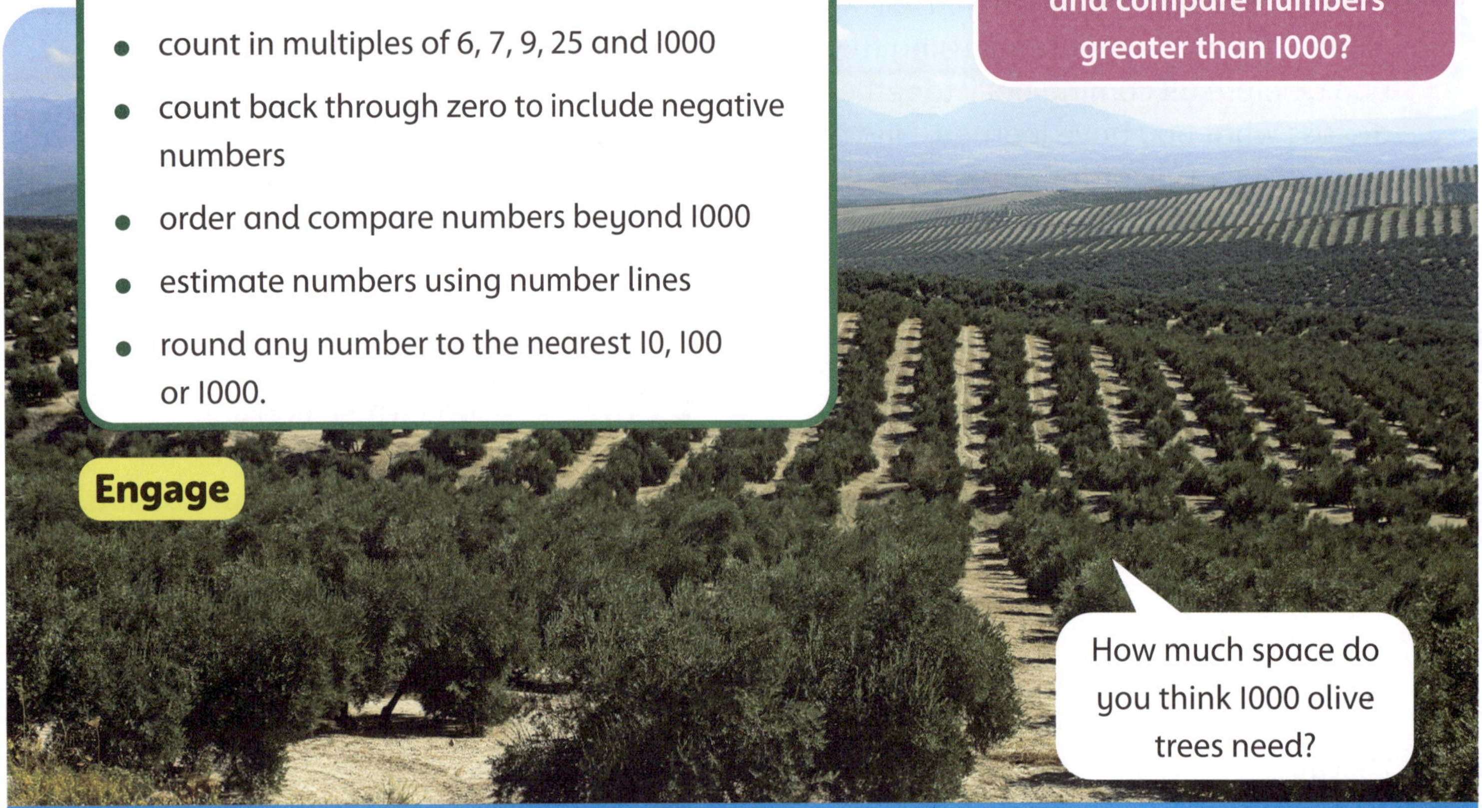

How much space do you think 1000 olive trees need?

How long do you think it takes to count to 1000?

How many jars do you think you need to have 1000 olives?

1A Place value and partitioning

Write numbers

Think back

The place or position of a digit in a number tells you its size or value.

In words, the number below is one thousand two hundred and seventy-four.

Thousands	Hundreds	Tens	Ones
1	2	7	4

Represents 1000	Represents 200	Represents 70	Represents 4 ones

When one of the places has no value we use a zero as a placeholder.

For example, in the number 3045, the zero shows that there are no hundreds.

In words, this number is three thousand and forty-five.

1 Write these numbers in numerals. The first one is done for you.

a Four thousand six hundred and thirty-four   4634

b One thousand three hundred and twelve

c Three thousand and sixty-nine

d Eight thousand three hundred and two

Can you think of a 4-digit number that has two zeros?

2 Write these numbers in words. The first one is done for you.

a 7169 _Seven thousand one hundred and sixty-nine_

b 4372 _____

c 3097 _____

d 5009 _____

Discover (continued)

3 Use these four digits to make:

$$7 \quad 4 \quad 9 \quad 1$$

a the largest number possible

b the largest even number possible

c the smallest number possible

d the smallest even number possible.

Check your answers with a partner.

4 Partition these numbers.

a 1857 = 1000 + ☐ + ☐ + 7

b 6382 = ☐ + 300 + ☐ + 2

c 9174 = ☐ + ☐ + 70 + ☐

d 7813 = ☐ + ☐ + ☐ + ☐

When you know the value of the digits, you can **partition** a number.
I can partition 2135:
2000 + 100 + 30 + 5

5 Partition these numbers.

a 1526 = ☐

b 4837 = ☐

c 3054 = ☐

d 7303 = ☐

Stretch zone

Can you explain to a partner how to partition 6007 and 8070?

■ For more practice, go to Practice Book 4, page 14.

1A Place value and partitioning

Explore

Write and round numbers

I   Estimate where each 4-digit number goes on the number line. Mark and label the number on the number line.

💬 ● Write the value of the digit that is <u>underlined</u>.

a <u>4</u>268

The underlined digit has a value of

_____

In <u>4</u>268, the underlined digit has a value of 4 thousands.

b 3<u>2</u>79

The underlined digit has a value of

_____

c 6<u>7</u>05

The underlined digit has a value of

_____

d 254<u>1</u>

The underlined digit has a value of

_____

Can you think of a number that has the same number of tens and thousands?
Can you think of a number that has the same number of ones and hundreds?

e 70<u>4</u>3

The underlined digit has a value of

_____

Explore (continued)

2 Use these numbers to make three 3-digit numbers.

| 400 | 300 | 70 | 2 | 100 | 8 | 90 | 7 | 800 |

- Mark and label your numbers on this number line.

378

0 ←——————|——————|————→ 1000

I made
300 + 70 + 8 = 378.

3 Round your numbers to the nearest 10.

378	is	380	to the nearest 10.
	is		to the nearest 10.
	is		to the nearest 10.
	is		to the nearest 10.

Remember: if a number ends in 5, round it up to the next multiple of 10.

4 Use these numbers to make three 4-digit numbers.

| 2000 | 60 | 300 | 4 | 80 | 7 | 500 | 3 |
| 8000 | 50 | 5 | 5000 | | | | |

- Mark and label your numbers on this number line.

2567

0 ←——————|——————|————→ 10000

I made 2000 + 500 + 60 + 7 = 2567.

5 Round your numbers to the nearest 100.

2567	is	2600	to the nearest 100.
	is		to the nearest 100.
	is		to the nearest 100.
	is		to the nearest 100.

If a number ends in 50, round it up to the next multiple of 100.

Stretch zone

Write a number that is 3500 to the nearest 100 and 3450 to the nearest 10.

■ For more practice, go to Practice Book 4, page 15.

1B Counting on and back

Discover

Use place value to count on and back

Key words
- count on
- count back

Think back

You can use place value to count on and count back in ones, tens, hundreds and thousands.

For example: 5642 + **100** = 5742   5742 + **1000** = 6742

6742 − **1** = 6741   6741 + **10** = 6751

Use the answer to each calculation as the start number in the next calculation.

1 Complete these steps.

a 2574 − **1000** = ☐

☐ + **100** = ☐

☐ + **10** = ☐

☐ − **1** = ☐

b 1099 + **1** = ☐

☐ + **1000** = ☐

☐ + **100** = ☐

☐ − **10** = ☐

2 Look at the numbers in the middle column of the table.

- Count on and back to complete both sides of the table. The first row is done for you.

	−1000	−100	−10	−1	Number	+1	+10	+100	+1000
	123	1123	1223	1233	**1234**	1235	1245	1345	2345
a					**3261**				
b					**4075**				
c					**2189**				
d					**5075**				
e					**5375**				

Stretch zone

What changes and what stays the same when you count on in 100s?
What changes and what stays the same when you count on in 1000s?

■ For more practice, go to Practice Book 4, page 16.

Explore

A number journey

1 Work with a partner.

- Choose a 3-digit number.

- Each of you write this number on your whiteboard. Then follow this number journey:

  - Add 2000

  - Take away 2

  - Add 200

  - Take away 10.

- Check your final answer with your partner. Did you both get the same number?

2 Write your own number journey using a 4-digit number. Make sure that every digit changes during your journey.

- Give your 4-digit number and the instructions for the number journey to your partner. Then check their answer.

3 The table shows some computer game scores.

Work out the difference between each start score and the new score.

Start score	New score	Difference
4560	4660	
2913	3113	
7521	9521	
1309	1349	
3189	4289	

Key words
- multiples of 10
- multiples of 100
- multiples of 1000

I chose 123. I made 2123, 2121, 2321, 2311.

Don't show your partner your whiteboard!

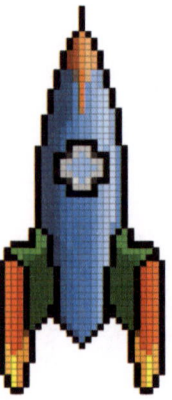

Stretch zone

Write three different pairs of numbers with a difference of 200.

12

■ For more practice, go to Practice Book 4, page 17.

1C Counting in multiples

Discover

Number sequences

1 Write the next four numbers in each sequence. The first number in each sequence is 1.

a The rule is 'add 6'. | 1 | | | | |

b The rule is 'add 7'. | 1 | | | | |

c The rule is 'add 9'. | 1 | | | | |

d The rule is 'add 25'. | 1 | | | | |

e The rule is 'add 1000'. | 1 | | | | |

If the rule is 'add 3', the sequence is 1, 4, 7, 10, 13.

2 Pick three cards from a set of digit cards 1–9.

- Use the digits to make a 3-digit start number.

- Write the number in the first box in each sequence.

- Then write the next four numbers in each sequence.

6   8   3

I picked 3, 6 and 8. I made the number 683.

a (add 6) | | | | | |

b (add 7) | | | | | |

c (add 9) | | | | | |

d (add 25) | | | | | |

e (add 1000) | | | | | |

Stretch zone

Write a sequence of five numbers that starts with 1 and ends with a number between 40 and 50. You must add the same number each time.

1 Number and place value

■ For more practice, go to Practice Book 4, page 18.

1C Counting in multiples

Explore

Key words
- multiple
- number sequence

Complete number sequences

1   Write four number sequences.

- You must count on or back in multiples of 6, 7, 9, 25 or 1000.

- Use any start number. Write the first five numbers in each sequence.

- Do not write the rule yet!

	Sequence	Rule
a		The rule is:
b		The rule is:
c		The rule is:
d		The rule is:

I chose 154 as my start number. My sequence is 154, 163, 172, 181, 190. Can you guess my rule?

I think your rule is 'add 9'. The next two numbers are 199 and 208.

2   Swap your number sequences with a partner.

- Write the rule for your partner's sequences. Then write the next two numbers in each sequence.

Stretch zone

Write a sequence that counts on in multiples of 25. Choose a start number between 50 and 75. Continue until you finish with a number between 550 and 575. How many numbers are there in your sequence?

14

Discover

Thermometer numbers

Look at the thermometer. The temperatures below zero are negative numbers.

1 **a** Talk to a partner about what you notice.

   b Write three things about the thermometer.

- _____

   _____

- _____

   _____

- _____

   _____

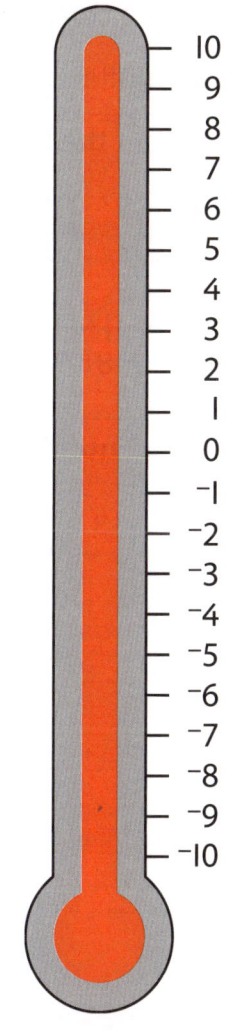

2 Count back in ones from 10 to ⁻10. Say the numbers aloud.

3 Use the thermometer to help you complete these sequences.

   a (Count back in twos)

   8 6 ☐ 2 ☐ ⁻2 ⁻4 ☐

   b (Count back in threes)

   8 5 ☐ ⁻1 ☐ ⁻7 ☐

   c (Count back in fours)

   10 ☐ 2 ☐ ☐ ⁻10

   d (Count on in 3s)

   ⁻12 ☐ ⁻6 ☐ ☐ 3

When we see ⁻7, we say **negative seven**.

Stretch zone

Write two counting-back sequences that start with 8 and end with ⁻10.

■ For more practice, go to Practice Book 4, page 20.

1D Negative numbers

Explore

 The answer is negative

Repeat these steps 10 times and complete the table below.

- Pick two cards from a set of digit cards 1–9.
- The smaller number is your start number.
- Subtract the larger number from your start number.

Key words
- negative number
- positive number

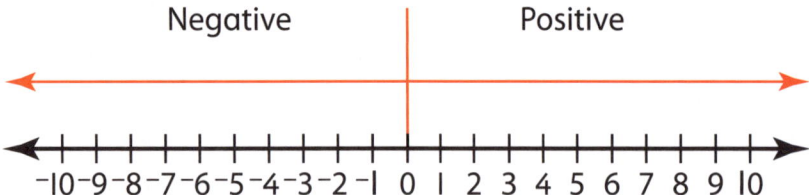

Negative   Positive

-10 -9 -8 -7 -6 -5 -4 -3 -2 -1 0 1 2 3 4 5 6 7 8 9 10

I picked 4 and 9. My start number was 4. I subtracted 9. I finished on ⁻5 (negative 5).

Start number	Subtract	Finish on
4	9	⁻5

Stretch zone

I count back 7 and finish on a negative number. Find a possible start number. What number did I finish on? How many different start and finish numbers can you find?

■ For more practice, go to Practice Book 4, page 21.

1E Roman numerals

Discover

Key word
● Roman numerals

Introducing Roman numerals

Did you know?

● We can use Roman numerals to write numbers. Roman numerals used these symbols:

  I, V, X, L, C, D and M.

● Roman numerals are sometimes used at the end of a TV programme or a film to show the date the programme was made.

● We sometimes see Roman numerals on clock faces.

How to read Roman numerals

Rules:

1 If a smaller numeral comes *after* a larger numeral, add the smaller numeral to the larger numeral. For example, XI: X + I is II

2 If a smaller numeral comes *before* a larger numeral, subtract the smaller numeral from the larger numeral. For example, IX: X − I is 9

3 Do not use the same numeral more than three times in a row. For example, VIII is 8 but IX is 9 (not VIIII).

Clues:

● The year 2020 in Roman numerals is MMXX.

● I am 6I years old today. My age in Roman numerals is LXI.

● The Roman Empire lasted for 507 years. This is DVII in Roman numerals.

● The maximum score in a game of darts is I80. This is CLXXX.

Use the rules and clues above to work out the value of these symbols.

I I ☐   2 V ☐   3 X ☐   4 L ☐   5 C ☐

Stretch zone

Some numbers have the same number of Roman numerals as digits 0–9. For example, 2020 is MMXX – both use 4 numerals or digits. Find three more numbers that have the same number of Roman numerals as digits 0–9.

■ For more practice, go to Practice Book 4, page 22.

1E Roman numerals

Explore

Write Roman numerals

1 What numbers do these Roman numerals represent?

Look back at the rules and clues on page 17 to help you.

a II

b IV

c IX

d XIV

e XVIII

f XIX

g LXIX

h CLXIX

i DCLXIX

j MDCLXIX

2 Write these numbers in Roman numerals.

a Your age

b The number of students in your class

c The number of students in your school

To write the Roman numerals for numbers bigger than 1000, you draw a horizontal bar over a numeral. This multiplies the value by 1000. For example, 100 000 is:

$\overline{\text{C}}$

 Stretch zone

Use Roman numerals to write the population of your town or city and the population of your country.

■ For more practice, go to Practice Book 4, page 23.

Connect

River lengths

The River Nile is the **longest** river in the world, from its source to its delta on the Mediterranean Sea.

The River Amazon is the world's **biggest** river, measured by the amount of water that flows down it. On average, the water that flows out of the mouth of the Amazon would fill 20 swimming pools every second!

Now it is your turn! Work in groups.

1 Research some rivers.

- Find ten of the world's longest rivers. They must be more than 1000 km long.

- For each river, find:

    a the length in kilometres

    b the countries or continent that the river flows through

    c an interesting numerical fact about the river.

2 Order your rivers from the longest to the shortest.

3 Round the lengths of your rivers to the nearest 10 km and the nearest 100 km.

4 Present your river facts in an interesting way.

Stretch zone

Talk to a partner about your river facts. What is the most interesting fact that your partner found?

1 Number and place value

Review

1   Write six different 4-digit numbers between 3000 and 5000.

- Do not use more than one zero in each number.

- Choose three odd numbers and three even numbers.

2   Write your numbers, in order, from smallest to largest.

Smallest ————————————————————→ Largest

3   Mark your numbers on the number line as accurately as you can.

←————————————|————————————→
  3000   5000

 4   Choose one of your numbers from **question 1** as a start number.

    a Count on in 25s. Write the next four numbers in the sequence.

        Start number

    b Count on in 1000s. Write the next four numbers in the sequence

        Start number

5   Use the last number in your sequence from **question 4b**.

Partition this number into thousands, hundreds, tens and ones.

 6   Hamad has 468 stickers in his collection. Somchai has 1002 more stickers than Hamad. Oliver has 72 fewer stickers than Somchai. How many stickers does Oliver have?

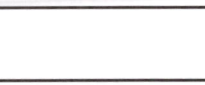

? What methods can I use to add and subtract numbers with up to 4 digits?

In this unit you will:

- add and subtract numbers with up to 4 digits
- estimate and use inverse operations to check answers to a calculation
- solve addition and subtraction problems.

When do you add and subtract numbers in everyday life?

Engage

Ziggy doubles her points. Is she now in 1st place?

How many more points does Drago need to equal 1st place?

How many more points does Ziggy have than Maths4ever?

How many points do Princess and RacingKing have in total?

What methods did you use?

How can you check your answers?

1st	SleepyJoe	8492
2nd	Drago	8056
3rd	Princess	7412
4th	RacingKing	6209
5th	Ziggy	4078
6th	Maths4ever	3645

2A Adding three or four small numbers

Discover

Add lots of numbers

Think back

In a magic square, the total of the numbers in each row, column and diagonal is the same.

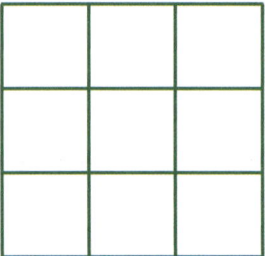

Column   Diagonal

Row

Key words
- bonds to 10
- vertical
- horizontal
- diagonal

1   Write these numbers in the magic square so that the total in every row, column and diagonal is 150.

10	20	30	40	50
60	70	80	90	

2   Write six additions with a total of 20. In each addition, use one number from each box below.

3	4	2
5	1	6
7	9	8

6	7	3
8	10	6
9	8	9

8	9	6
5	11	10
9	7	4

Cross out the numbers as you use them. You can use each number only once.

- Write your calculations here.

Stretch zone

Repeat **question 2**, but this time try to write nine additions with a total of 20. It is possible!

■ For more practice, go to Practice Book 4, page 25.

2A Adding three or four small numbers

Explore

Strategies for adding lots of numbers

Key words
- bridging 10
- number bonds to 10 and 20
- commutativity

Think back

You can look for number bonds to 10 or 20 to help you add lots of small numbers.

For example, you can add 3, 8 and 17 like this:

3 + 17 = 20
20 + 8 = 28
so 3 + 8 + 17 = 28

1   How many different ways can you make 18 by adding three single-digit numbers?

I added 1, 8 and 9 to make 18. I know that 1 + 9 = 10, so I wrote:
1 + 9 + 8 = 18.

2   Look at your number sentences in **question 1**. Underline all the number bonds to 10.

3   Add each set of numbers mentally.

a 15, 2, 5, 9 ☐   **d** 5, 6, 7, 4 ☐

b 8, 7, 4, 2 ☐   **e** 9, 3, 7, 4 ☐

c 8, 9, 5, 2 ☐   **f** 8, 7, 12, 3 ☐

Compare your additions with a partner. Did you both find all the possible additions?

Stretch zone

Use three of these numbers to make a total less than 25. How many additions can you write in 5 minutes?

16	7	13	2
11	4	18	5

2 Addition and subtraction

23

■ For more practice, go to Practice Book 4, page 26.

Discover

Find sums and differences

1 Work with a partner. Choose four cards from a set of 0–9 digit cards. Use the cards to make two 2-digit numbers. Work individually to calculate:

   a the **sum** of the two numbers

   b the **difference** between the two numbers

   c the sum of answer **a** and answer **b**

   d half of answer **c**.

I made 45 and 76. The sum is **121**. The difference is **31**.

The sum of my two answers is **152**. Half of 152 is **76**.

2 Did you both get the same answers? Check your answers using inverse calculations.

   a

   b

   c

   d

3 Repeat the activity with three more pairs of numbers.

4 What do you notice about your answers each time?

   _____

   _____

Stretch zone

Choose three different pairs of numbers with a difference of 26. Repeat steps **a**–**d** from **question 1**. What do you notice about the answers for each pair of numbers?

■ For more practice, go to Practice Book 4, page 27.

2B Adding or subtracting 2-digit numbers

Strategies for adding and subtracting

Key words
- partitioning
- sum
- counting on
- difference

1 Work out these additions. They all involve adding 56.

Worked example

You can use place-value counters to add two numbers.

● = 1s
● = 10s
● = 100s

Exchange 10 ones for 1 ten
Exchange 10 tens for 1 hundred

45 + 56 = 101

Another method is to use partitioning. First I added 50 and then added 6.
45 + 50 = 95, then 95 + 6 = 101

a 67 + 56 = ☐

b 82 + 56 = ☐

c 39 + 56 = ☐

d 99 + 56 = ☐

e 58 + 56 = ☐

2 Work out these additions. They all involve adding 68.

a 37 + 68 = ☐

b 76 + 68 = ☐

c 29 + 68 = ☐

d 95 + 68 = ☐

e 97 + 68 = ☐

I used partitioning too. I changed 37 + 68 to 37 + 60 + 8.

2B Adding or subtracting 2-digit numbers

Explore (continued)

Think back

To work out a subtraction, we can use a number line to count on from the smaller number to the larger number.

74 − 28 = 46

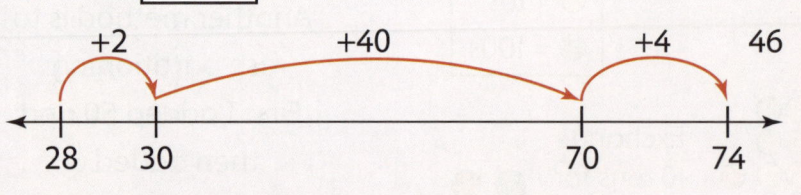

I can check 74 − 28 = 46 by adding. 28 + 46 = 74, so I know the answer is correct.

3 Use a number line method to complete each subtraction.

Write an addition to check each answer.

a 65 − 27 = ☐   Check: ☐ + ☐ = ☐

b 80 − 43 = ☐   Check: ☐ + ☐ = ☐

c 82 − 46 = ☐   Check: ☐ + ☐ = ☐

d 92 − 46 = ☐   Check: ☐ + ☐ = ☐

Stretch zone

How can you use your answer to **question 3c** to work out **question 3d**?

■ For more practice, go to Practice Book 4, page 28.

2C Mental addition and subtraction

Discover

Add and subtract near multiples

1 Work with a partner.

- Write four different 3-digit numbers.

- One person adds 199 to each number.

- The other person adds 201 to each number.

- Record your answers in this table.

Our numbers	I added _____	My partner added _____

2 Compare your answers. What do you notice?

_____

_____

3 What is an easy way to do each of the calculations below?

- Write the steps of each calculation.

To add 13: _____

To add 99: _____

To add 197: _____

To take away 302: _____

Key words

- near multiple of 10
- near multiple of 100
- near double

To add 199, I **add** 200 and then **take away** 1.

To add 201, I **add** 200 and then **add** an extra 1.

To take away 8, the steps are: − 10 + 2

Stretch zone

Describe your strategy for subtracting 98 from a number. Show that it works by writing two example calculations.

2 Addition and subtraction

27

Explore

Near multiple strategies

1 Complete this table. The first one is done for you.

Number	+ 109
246	355
572	
838	
153	
625	
497	
364	
789	

To add 109, I **add** 110 then **take away** 1.

For example:
246 + 109 = 355
(246 + 110 = 356, then 356 − 1)

2 Complete this table. The first one is done for you.

Number	− 101
627	526
355	
784	
462	
279	
848	
191	
533	

To take away 101, I **take away** 100 then **take away** 1

For example:
627 − 101 = 526
(627 − 100 = 527, then 527 − 1)

2C Mental addition and subtraction

Explore (continued)

3 Work out the additions and complete the table.

+	11	31	149	151	129
646					
483					
738					

4 Use a number line to work out these subtractions.

a 365 − 198 = [ ]

b 509 − 198 = [ ]

c 209 − 198 = [ ]

5 Describe to a partner your strategy for taking away 198.

6 Use a number line to work out these additions.

a 374 + 103 = [ ]

b 824 + 103 = [ ]

c 825 + 103 = [ ]

7 Describe to a partner your strategy for adding 103.

Stretch zone

Describe your strategy for subtracting 297 from a number. Show that it works by writing two example calculations.

■ For more practice, go to Practice Book 4, page 30.

Discover

Introducing column addition

Worked example

There are 394 students in the local primary school and 853 in the secondary school. How many students are there in total?

	Thousands	Hundreds	Tens	Ones
394				
853				
1247				

Key words
- column addition
- regrouping

You can model the problem using base-10 equipment.

I estimated the answer first, by rounding to the nearest 10: $390 + 850 = 1240$

Use column addition to answer these word problems.

1   462 people went to a funfair on Friday. 735 people went on Saturday. How many people went altogether on Friday and Saturday?

2   A shop has two large crates of bananas. There are 652 bananas in one crate and 587 in the other. How many bananas are there altogether?

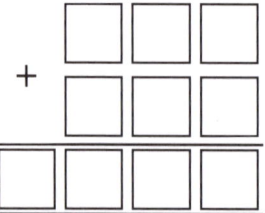

Stretch zone

Twice as many people visit Sunshine Beach as visit Surf Beach. If 482 people visit Surf Beach, how many go to the two beaches altogether?

30

2D Written methods of addition

Explore 1

Write column additions

I Use the digits 5, 6, 7 and 8 to make four pairs of 3- or 4-digit numbers.

- Add each pair of numbers.
- Estimate your answer first.

Key word
- column addition
- regrouping

I made 586 and 6758. I estimated my answer first by rounding each number to the nearest hundred: $600 + 6800 = 7400$

Worked example

Step 1

```
   5 8 6
+ 6 7 5 8
─────────
         4
   I
```

First I added the ones. I regrouped 14 ones into I ten and 4 ones.

Step 2

```
   5 8 6
+ 6 7 5 8
─────────
       4 4
   I I
```

Then I added the tens. I regrouped 14 tens into I hundred and 4 tens.

Step 3

```
   5 8 6
+ 6 7 5 8
─────────
     3 4 4
   I I I
```

I added the hundreds. 13 hundreds is I thousand and 3 hundreds.

Step 4

```
   5 8 6
+ 6 7 5 8
─────────
   7 3 4 4
   I I I
```

I added the thousands.

Stretch zone

What is the largest possible total of a 3-digit and a 4-digit number made using all the digits 2, 3, 4, 5, 6, 7, 8?

■ For more practice, go to Practice Book 4, page 32.

2D Written methods of addition

Explore 2

Key words
- column addition
- regrouping
- mass

Addition word problems

This table shows some of the heaviest land mammals.

Animal	African elephant	Asian elephant	White rhinoceros	Indian rhinoceros	Water buffalo
Mass in kg	6246	3152	2184	2070	488

I Use a written method to calculate the answers to these questions. Show all your workings in the grid.

Estimate your answers first.

a The total mass of an African and an Asian elephant.

Estimate:

b The total mass of an Indian and a white rhinoceros.

Estimate:

c The total mass of an African elephant and a water buffalo.

Estimate:

d The total mass of an Indian rhinoceros and a water buffalo.

Estimate:

 2 Check each of your answers using a subtraction.

 **Stretch zone**

What is the total mass of all five animals?

■ For more practice, go to Practice Book 4, page 33.

2E Written methods of subtraction

Discover

Introducing column subtraction

Use a column subtraction to answer these word problems.

Key words
- subtraction
- column method
- regrouping

Worked example

A shop sells goods worth $3257 in a week. The shopkeeper has to pay bills of $1162 each week. How much money does the shopkeeper have left at the end of the week?

Thousands	Hundreds	Tens	Ones
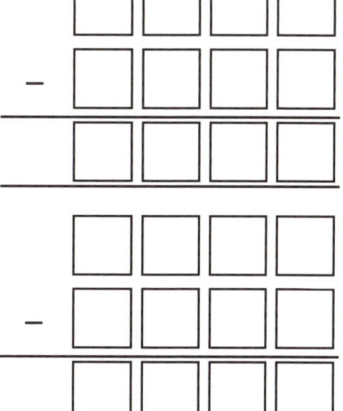			

I use blocks, rods and cubes to represent 3257. I need to subtract 1162.

I regroup 1 hundred into 10 tens.

When I subtract 1162 I have 2095 left.

$3257 – $1162 = $2095

You can model the problems using base-10 equipment.

I estimated the answer first, by rounding to the nearest 100:
3300 – 1200 = 2100

1 There are 1157 people at the theatre. At the interval 215 people leave. How many people are still in the theatre?

2 A shop has 1342 melons. It sells 452 melons during the week. How many melons does the shop have left at the end of the week?

Stretch zone

Write a subtraction word problem with the answer 1867. Show how to solve your word problem.

■ For more practice, go to Practice Book 4, page 34.

2 Addition and subtraction

Explore 1

Write column subtractions

Use the digits 5, 6, 7 and 8 to make four pairs of 3- or 4-digit numbers.

- Subtract the smaller number from the larger number in each pair.

- Estimate your answer first.

I made 5768 and 685.
I estimated my
answer first:
5800 – 700 = 5100

Worked example

Step 1

$$\begin{array}{r} 5\,7\,6\,8 \\ -\ \ 6\,8\,5 \\ \hline 3 \end{array}$$

First I subtracted the ones. 8 – 5 = 3. No regrouping was necessary.

Step 2

$$\begin{array}{r} 5\,{}^{6}\!\!\not7\,{}^{1}6\,8 \\ -\ \ 6\,8\,5 \\ \hline 8\,3 \end{array}$$

I exchanged 1 hundred for 10 tens so that I had 16 tens. I then subtracted the tens. 16 – 8 = 8.

Step 3

$$\begin{array}{r} 5\,{}^{6}\!\!\not7\,{}^{1}6\,8 \\ -\ \ 6\,8\,5 \\ \hline 0\,8\,3 \end{array}$$

I subtracted the hundreds. 6 – 6 = 0.

Step 4

$$\begin{array}{r} 5\,{}^{6}\!\!\not7\,{}^{1}6\,8 \\ -\ \ 6\,8\,5 \\ \hline 5\,0\,8\,3 \end{array}$$

Finally, I subtracted the thousands.

Stretch zone

What is the smallest possible difference between a 3-digit and a 4-digit number made using all the digits 2, 3, 4, 5, 6, 7, 8?

■ For more practice, go to Practice Book 4, page 35.

2E Written methods of subtraction

Explore 2

Subtraction problems

This table shows some of the heaviest land mammals.

Animal	African elephant	Asian elephant	White rhinoceros	Indian rhinoceros	Water buffalo

Mass in kg	6246	3152	2184	2070	488

I Use a written method to calculate the answers to these questions. Show all your workings in the grids.

Estimate your answers first.

a The difference in mass between an African and an Asian elephant.

b The difference in mass between a white and an Indian rhinoceros.

c The difference in mass between an African elephant and a water buffalo.

d The difference in mass between an Indian rhinoceros and a water buffalo.

 2 Check each of your answers using an addition.

 **Stretch zone**

What is the difference between the combined mass of the two elephants and the combined mass of the two rhinos?

■ For more practice, go to Practice Book 4, page 36.

Connect

Add and subtract city distances

This table gives information about the direct distances between some cities around the world.

Imagine you want to travel between some different cities.

	Distance (kilometres)
London to Bangkok	9544
London to San Francisco	8640
London to Sao Paulo	9470
Sao Paulo to Bogota	4310
Sao Paulo to Mexico City	7423
Sao Paulo to Paris	9376
Paris to London	454
Paris to Bogota	8632
Paris to Bangkok	9457
Bangkok to Melbourne	7355
Bangkok to New Delhi	2917
Bangkok to Abu Dhabi	4975

I can use mental and written methods to add and subtract numbers with up to 4 digits. I can use base-10 equipment and number lines to help me.

I want to travel from London to Sao Paulo and then to Mexico City. I need to work out 9470 + 7423.

1 Write three journeys involving three or four cities. Work out the total distance for each journey.

a _____

   _____ ☐ km

b _____

   _____ ☐ km

c _____

   _____ ☐ km

The distance between two cities is the same in the other direction. For example, the journey from Bangkok to London is 9544 km.

2 Use your journeys to answer these questions:

a What is the total distance of all your journeys? ☐ km

b What is the difference between your longest journey and your shortest journey? ☐ km

Stretch zone

Choose four cities from the table. Find the shortest journey that goes to all of these cities.

2 Addition and subtraction

Review

Here is some data about a film shown at the local cinema.

	Number of tickets sold	Ticket sales ($)	Snack sales ($)
Monday	323	3230	1432
Tuesday	415	4150	2487
Wednesday	489	4890	2356
Thursday	623	6230	3709

Use the data in the table to answer the questions. Show your workings.

1 How many tickets were sold altogether on Monday and Tuesday?

2 How much more money was made from ticket sales than from snack sales on Thursday?

3 How much more money was made from snack sales on Wednesday than on Monday?

4 Write two more addition and subtraction questions about this data.

   a _____

        _____

   b _____

        _____

3 Multiplication and division

? How can I multiply and divide numbers?

In this unit you will:

- recall multiplication and division facts to 12 × 12
- multiply and divide mentally
- recognise and use factor pairs in mental calculations
- multiply 2- and 3-digit numbers using written methods
- solve multiplication problems.

Engage

Work with a partner.

You have $1000 to spend on fish for a new aquarium.

How many of each fish you will you buy?

Red tail botia $14	Zebra stripe $7	Polka dot botia $9	Yellow tail botia $11
Red tail zebra $13	Doctor garra $6	Tiger botia $8	Dwarf chain botia $12

Choose a minimum of 10 of each type of fish.

Work out the cost.

Use paper for planning. Make a clear list of your final choices, showing the number and cost of each type of fish.

Discover

Patterns in multiplication tables

Use the 100-square below.

Key words
- multiple
- even
- odd

1 Colour the multiples of 2 yellow.

1	2	3	4	5	6	7	8	9	10
11	12	13	14	15	16	17	18	19	20
21	22	23	24	25	26	27	28	29	30
31	32	33	34	35	36	37	38	39	40
41	42	43	44	45	46	47	48	49	50
51	52	53	54	55	56	57	58	59	60
61	62	63	64	65	66	67	68	69	70
71	72	73	74	75	76	77	78	79	80
81	82	83	84	85	86	87	88	89	90
91	92	93	94	95	96	97	98	99	100

Write a description of the pattern.

_____

_____

2 On the same 100-square, colour the multiples of 4 orange.

Describe the new pattern.

_____

_____

3 Now colour the multiples of 8 red.

Describe this pattern.

_____

_____

Use the key words
and these words
to help you:
column, row, vertical,
alternate.

Discover (continued)

The multiples of 3, 6 and 9 give a new family of patterns.

4 Colour the multiples of 3 green, the multiples of 6 blue and the multiples of 9 purple.

1	2	3	4	5	6	7	8	9	10
11	12	13	14	15	16	17	18	19	20
21	22	23	24	25	26	27	28	29	30
31	32	33	34	35	36	37	38	39	40
41	42	43	44	45	46	47	48	49	50
51	52	53	54	55	56	57	58	59	60
61	62	63	64	65	66	67	68	69	70
71	72	73	74	75	76	77	78	79	80
81	82	83	84	85	86	87	88	89	90
91	92	93	94	95	96	97	98	99	100

5 Describe the patterns you can see for the multiples of 3, 6 and 9.

Multiples of 3: _____

_____

Multiples of 6: _____

_____

Multiples of 9: _____

_____

Use these words to help you: multiple, even, odd, diagonal, alternate, left, right, sloping.

Stretch zone

Make a poster that describes all the patterns you have found. Explain why the multiples make these patterns.

■ For more practice, go to Practice Book 4, page 38.

3A Multiplication tables and multiples

Explore 1

Multiplication facts

Key words
- multiply by 0
- multiply by 1

1 Complete these multiplications.

   a $6 \times 8 =$ ☐

   b $5 \times 12 =$ ☐

   c $8 \times 0 =$ ☐

   d $9 \times 3 =$ ☐

   e $4 \times 11 =$ ☐

   f $10 \times 1 =$ ☐

What happens when you multiply a number by 0?

What happens when you multiply a number by 1?

2 Write the missing numbers.

   a $5 \times$ ☐ $= 20$

   b $6 \times$ ☐ $= 36$

   c ☐ $\times 4 = 32$

   d $8 \times$ ☐ $= 88$

   e $3 \times$ ☐ $= 0$

   f ☐ $\times 9 = 9$

3 Find the **smallest** number that is:

   a a multiple of 2 and 3 ☐

   b a multiple of 3 and 5 ☐

   c a multiple of 4 and 5 ☐

   d a multiple of 10 and 4 ☐

   e a multiple of 9 and 5 ☐

   f a multiple of 6 and 4. ☐

4 Write five multiples of each number: 5, 10 and 100.

- Use the digits in the box and as many 0s as you like.
- You must include some 3-digit numbers.

| 3 | | 5 | | 7 |
| | 2 | | 6 | 4 |

   a 5 ☐ ☐ ☐ ☐ ☐

   b 10 ☐ ☐ ☐ ☐

   c 100 ☐ ☐ ☐ ☐ ☐

 **Stretch zone**

Explain how you know that your answers to **question 4** are correct.

■ For more practice, go to Practice Book 4, page 39.

3A Multiplication tables and multiples

Explore 2

Compare multiplication tables

Key words
- multiples
- factors
- digits

1 Write three numbers in each section of these Venn diagrams, including the intersections.

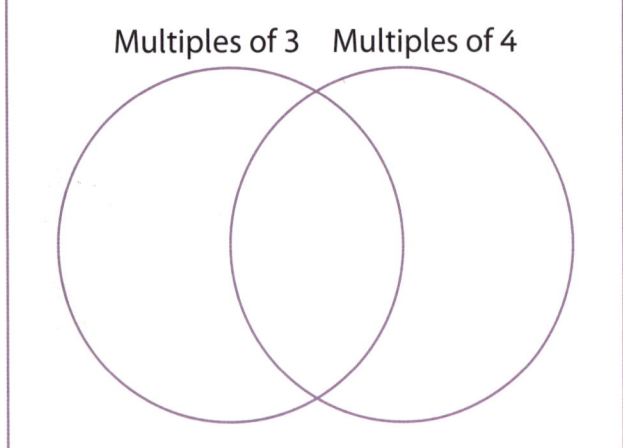

Multiples of 3   Multiples of 4

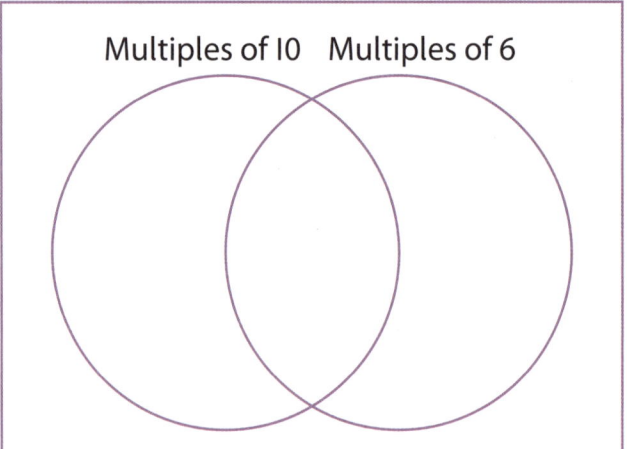

Multiples of 10   Multiples of 6

2 Look at these multiples of 4.   4, 8, 12, 16, 20, 24, 28, 32, 36, 40, …

   a Write the next five multiples.

   b Describe the pattern.

   _____

   _____

Does the pattern continue?

3 Read these statements. Circle true or false.

   a All multiples of 10 are also multiples of 5.   True / False

   b All multiples of 4 are also multiples of 3.   True / False

   c All multiples of 4 are even numbers.   True / False

   d All multiples of 3 are odd numbers.   True / False

   e If I multiply by 0 the answer is always 1.   True / False

   f If I multiply by 1 the answer is always 1.   True / False

Explain to a partner why each false statement is incorrect.

Stretch zone

Write the first ten multiples of 6. Can you spot any patterns? What patterns can you spot in other multiplication tables?

■ For more practice, go to Practice Book 4, page 40.

3B Doubling and halving

Discover

Doubling and halving strategies

Think back

Remember: doubling is the same as multiplying by 2.

To double a 2-digit number, we can split the number into tens and ones to make the doubling easier. Look at the example in the box.

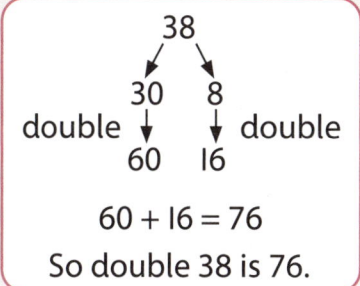

$$38$$
$$30 \quad 8$$
double ↓ ↓ double
$$60 \quad 16$$
$$60 + 16 = 76$$
So double 38 is 76.

I **Double** these numbers by doubling the tens, doubling the ones, then recombining.

a Double 43 ☐   **c** Double 58 ☐

b Double 19 ☐   **d** Double 75 ☐

2 **Halve** these numbers by halving the tens, halving the ones, then recombining.

a Halve 66 ☐   **c** Halve 44 ☐

b Halve 36 ☐   **d** Halve 54 ☐

3 Complete the table.

Type of shoe	Shoes	Slippers	Trainers	Sandals	Boots
Cost of I shoe		$21	$55		$48
Cost of a pair of shoes	$56			$38	

Stretch zone

How can you calculate the cost of 8 pairs of sandals?

■ For more practice, go to Practice Book 4, page 41.

3B Doubling and halving

Explore

Return journeys

The journey by air from Dubai to Muscat is 380 km.

The return journey from Dubai to Muscat to Dubai is double the distance: 760 km.

Key words
- double
- halve
- return journey

1 Write the length of each return journey.

Journey	Return journey
340 km	
180 km	
420 km	
270 km	
490 km	
360 km	

You can partition each number into hundreds and tens to make it easier to double. Then recombine.

2 Use doubling facts to help you calculate these near doubles.

a Double 42 = ☐   43 + 42 = ☐

b Double 28 = ☐   28 + 29 = ☐

c Double 47 = ☐   47 + 46 = ☐

d Double 36 = ☐   37 + 36 = ☐

Stretch zone

Research the lengths of three more journeys, between cities in different countries. Write the length of each return journey.

44

■ For more practice, go to Practice Book 4, page 42.

Discover

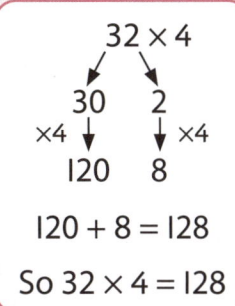 **Use different strategies to multiply**

Think back

To multiply a 2-digit number by a I-digit number, we can:

- partition the 2-digit number into tens and ones
- then multiply both parts by the I-digit number.

$$32 \times 4$$

30   2

×4 ↓   ↓ ×4

120   8

$120 + 8 = 128$

So $32 \times 4 = 128$

I Multiply these numbers by partitioning the 2-digit number into tens and ones, then recombining.

a 56 × 3 = (☐ × ☐) + (☐ × ☐) = ☐ + ☐ = ☐

b 44 × 5 = (☐ × ☐) + (☐ × ☐) = ☐ + ☐ = ☐

c 28 × 6 = (☐ × ☐) + (☐ × ☐) = ☐ + ☐ = ☐

d 53 × 9 = (☐ × ☐) + (☐ × ☐) = ☐ + ☐ = ☐

e 87 × 2 = (☐ × ☐) + (☐ × ☐) = ☐ + ☐ = ☐

f 34 × 6 = (☐ × ☐) + (☐ × ☐) = ☐ + ☐ = ☐

2 Use the answers from **question** I to help you work out these multiplications.

a 56 × 6 = ☐

b 44 × 10 = ☐

c 28 × 3 = ☐

d 53 × I = ☐

e 87 × 4 = ☐

f 34 × 0 = ☐

Discover (continued)

Think back

You can use the grid method to calculate 6×47.

×	40	7
6	240	42

240 + 42

Answer: $6 \times 47 =$ 282

3 Use the grid method to work out these multiplications.

a 4×58

×		

☐ + ☐

Answer: $4 \times 58 =$ ☐

b 3×85

×		

☐ + ☐

Answer: $3 \times 85 =$ ☐

c 64×5

×		

☐ + ☐

Answer: $64 \times 5 =$ ☐

d 35×9

×		

☐ + ☐

Answer: $35 \times 9 =$ ☐

e 60×73

×	70	3
60		

☐ + ☐

Answer: $60 \times 73 =$ ☐

f 70×74

×		

☐ + ☐

Answer: $70 \times 74 =$ ☐

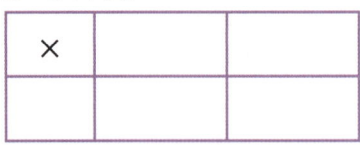

Stretch zone

Think of a difficult multiplication that you cannot solve mentally. Give it to a partner to solve using the grid method.

■ For more practice, go to Practice Book 4, page 43.

3C Multiplying 2-digit numbers

Explore

Multiply to find how much

These are the prices of some drinks in a cafe.

Key words
- 2-digit number
- product
- total cost

Orange juice	Can of cola	Lemon squash	Lemonade
59¢	45¢	63¢	57¢
Pineapple juice	Bottle of sparkling water	Blackcurrant squash	Lime juice
76¢	68¢	54¢	39¢

 Calculate the cost of the following orders. Use a method of your choice.

a 6 glasses of orange juice _____

b 5 cans of cola _____

c 7 glasses of lemon squash _____

d 4 glasses of lemonade _____

e 3 glasses of pineapple juice _____

f 8 bottles of sparkling water _____

g 9 glasses of blackcurrant squash _____

h 2 glasses of lime juice _____

 **Stretch zone**

Write a two-step problem using the drinks prices above. Give your problem to a partner to solve.

3 Multiplication and division

47

For more practice, go to Practice Book 4, page 44.

Discover

Different multiplications, same answer

This array shows $3 \times 8 = 24$.

1 Make four different arrays for 24, using counters. Write the multiplication that each array shows.

[ ] × [ ] = 24		[ ] × [ ] = 24
[ ] × [ ] = 24		[ ] × [ ] = 24

3 and 8 are factors of 24. Because $3 \times 8 = 24$ they are a **factor pair**.

2 Write four different multiplications with the answer 36 and four different multiplications with the answer 60.

[ ] × [ ] = 36		[ ] × [ ] = 60
[ ] × [ ] = 36		[ ] × [ ] = 60
[ ] × [ ] = 36		[ ] × [ ] = 60
[ ] × [ ] = 36		[ ] × [ ] = 60

How can arrays help you to work out all these calculations?

3 Solve these calculations by doubling one number and halving the other. One is done for you.

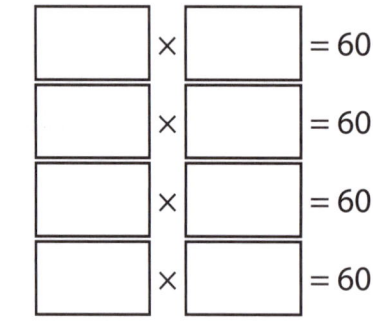

a 18×4 becomes $\boxed{36 \times 2} = \boxed{72}$

b 27×4 becomes $\boxed{} = \boxed{}$

c 13×4 becomes $\boxed{} = \boxed{}$

d 26×4 becomes $\boxed{} = \boxed{}$

e 28×4 becomes $\boxed{} = \boxed{}$

f 30×4 becomes $\boxed{} = \boxed{}$

I know that 18×4 is the same as 36×2. I doubled the first number and halved the second number.

Stretch zone

Can you explain the pattern in your answers to **questions 3d–f**?

■ For more practice, go to Practice Book 4, page 45.

3D Multiplication strategies

Explore

Change the order to multiply

1 Complete each multiplication in two ways.

Worked example

$5 \times 3 \times 2$

| 5 | × | 3 | = | 15 | and | 15 | × | 2 | = | 30 |

| 5 | × | 2 | = | 10 | and | 10 | × | 3 | = | 30 |

Key words

- multiply
- order
- commutative law
- associative law

Underline the numbers that you multiply first.

a $10 \times 4 \times 3$

| | × | | = | | and | | × | | = | |

| | × | | = | | and | | × | | = | |

b $2 \times 7 \times 5$

| | × | | = | | and | | × | | = | |

| | × | | = | | and | | × | | = | |

c $5 \times 10 \times 4$

| | × | | = | | and | | × | | = | |

| | × | | = | | and | | × | | = | |

d $4 \times 6 \times 3$

| | × | | = | | and | | × | | = | |

| | × | | = | | and | | × | | = | |

2 For each question in **question** 1, tick ✓ the way you found easier or quicker.

Stretch zone

Calculate $2 \times 8 \times 5 \times 3$. Explain your strategy to a partner.

3 Multiplication and division

49

■ For more practice, go to Practice Book 4, page 46.

Discover

Column multiplication

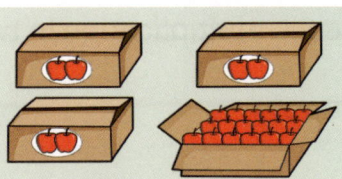

Worked example

I have 4 boxes with 24 apples in each box.
How many apples do I have altogether?

Tens	Ones	Number
		80 + 16
8 tens	16 ones	96

```
   2 4
×    4
   9 6
   1
```

16 ones is the same as 1 ten and 6 ones.

We write the 6 in the ones column and we write the 1 ten below the tens column.

So, 4 × 24 = 8 tens + 1 ten + 6 ones = 96

Use the column method to solve these word problems.

1 There are 5 coaches with 27 people on each coach.

   How many people are there in total?

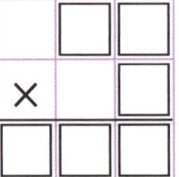

You can use base-10 equipment to model the problem.

2 I have 6 boxes of pencils. There are 45 pencils in each box.

   How many pencils do I have altogether?

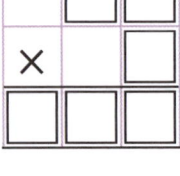

3 A box of cherries contains 36 cherries.

   How many cherries are there in 9 boxes?

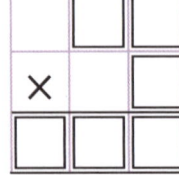

Stretch zone

How can you calculate the answer to **question 3** mentally?

■ For more practice, go to Practice Book 4, page 47.

3E Written methods for multiplication

Explore 1

Choose a method to multiply

Think back

We can use the grid method or the column method to calculate 256×3.

$$\begin{array}{r} 2\ 5\ 6 \\ \times \quad\ 3 \\ \hline 7\ 6\ 8 \\ 1\ 1 \end{array}$$

×	3
200	600
50	150
6	18
Total	768

Key words
- column method
- recombine

Remember to estimate the answer first. I know that 250×3 is 750, so the answer will be a bit more than 750.

Use any method to calculate these products.

- Show your workings.

1   $173 \times 5 = $ ☐

Estimate: _____

3   $186 \times 4 = $ ☐

Estimate: _____

2   $258 \times 3 = $ ☐

Estimate: _____

4   $143 \times 6 = $ ☐

Estimate: _____

Stretch zone

Do you prefer the grid method or the column method? Explain why to a partner. Use one of the calculations above to help you explain.

3 Multiplication and division

■ For more practice, go to Practice Book 4, page 48.

3E Written methods for multiplication

Explore 2

Multiplication problems

Use the grid method or column method to solve each problem.

- Show your workings.

1 A library has 283 bookshelves.
   Each bookshelf holds
   9 books.

   How many books does
   the library hold altogether?

   Estimate:

   _____

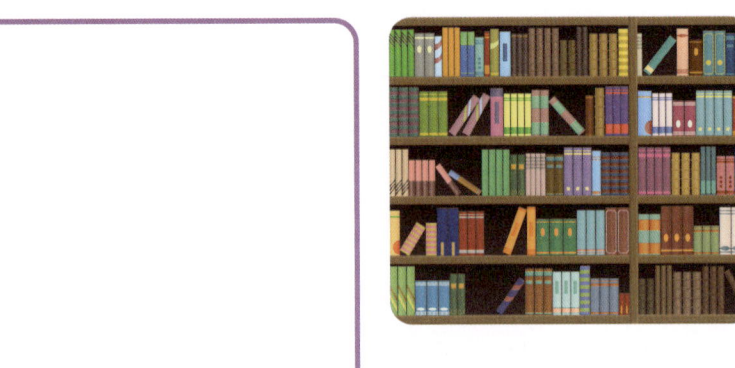

2 There are 48 teams in a mini-
   soccer tournament. Each team
   brings a squad of 8 players.

   How many players are
   there altogether?

   Estimate:

   _____

3 A farmer can plant
   478 cabbages in a field.
   The farmer has 9 fields.

   How many cabbages can
   the farmer plant altogether?

   Estimate:

   _____

Stretch zone

Write a multiplication word problem. Swap problems with a partner.
Use the column method to solve your partner's problem.

■ For more practice, go to Practice Book 4, page 49.

3F Dividing 2-digit numbers by a single-digit number

Discover 1

Investigate remainders

1 Complete this table. Some are done for you.

	31	32	33	34	35	36	37	38	39	40
÷ 3	10 r1									
÷ 4		8								
÷ 5			6 r3							
÷ 6				5 r4						
÷ 1										

2 Describe any patterns you can see in the table.

_____

_____

What is the result of dividing by 1? Can you explain why?

3 What is the largest remainder that you can have when you:

a divide by 3? ☐

b divide by 4? ☐

c divide by 6? ☐

d divide by 9? ☐

4 Choose one number from each box.

- Write a division calculation with your two numbers.
- Solve the division.

| 71 | 67 | 87 | 59 | 79 | | 6 | 3 | 4 | 9 |

Use a number line and your knowledge of times tables to help you.

Stretch zone

Write a division word problem with an answer that has remainder 4.

3 Multiplication and division

■ For more practice, go to Practice Book 4, page 50.

Discover 2

Use chunking to divide

Key words
- division
- divisor
- remainder

Think back

When we use chunking, we write the calculation vertically.

For example: What is $93 \div 6$?

10 lots of 6 + 5 lots of 6 = 90. We have a remainder of 3.

$$
\begin{array}{rl}
93 & \\
-60 & \quad 10 \times 6 \\
\hline
33 & \\
-30 & \quad 5 \times 6 \\
\hline
3 & \quad r\,3
\end{array}
$$

$93 \div 6 = 15\,r\,3$

I need to write all the numbers down very carefully.

Use the chunking method to solve these calculations.

1 $69 \div 4$

2 $89 \div 4$

3 $61 \div 4$

4 $70 \div 6$

Stretch zone

How can you tell what the remainder will be before you calculate $61 \div 4$?

■ For more practice, go to Practice Book 4, page 51.

Explore

Division problems

Solve these problems mentally. Use multiplication facts that you know.

You can use the chunking method if you prefer.

1 There are 5 chocolate biscuits in a pack.

   You need 80 biscuits for a party.

   How many packs do you need to buy?

   I need to buy ⬚ packs of biscuits.

chocolate biscuits

2 You have 96 stickers.

   You can put 6 stickers on a page.

   How many pages can you fill?

   I can fill ⬚ pages.

3 4 children can fit in a canoe.

   How many canoes do we need for 60 children?

   We need ⬚ canoes.

4 There are 95 chairs in a hall.

   The chairs are in groups of 5.

   How many groups of chairs are there?

   There are ⬚ groups of chairs.

5 There are 144 students in my school. In the school canteen, 8 students can sit at each table. How many tables do we need?

   We need ⬚ tables.

Explore (continued)

6 Choose a 2-digit number from this section of the 100-square.

- Circle your chosen number.

81	82	83	84	85	86	87	88	89	90
91	92	93	94	95	96	97	98	99	100

- Divide your number by 2, 3, 4, 5, 6, 9 and 10.

- Use this box for your workings. Write the answers below.

You can use any method. You may be able to do some of the divisions mentally.

☐ ÷ 2 = ☐   ☐ ÷ 6 = ☐

☐ ÷ 3 = ☐   ☐ ÷ 9 = ☐

☐ ÷ 4 = ☐   ☐ ÷ 10 = ☐

☐ ÷ 5 = ☐

- How many of your calculations have a remainder? ☐

Stretch zone

Can you find a number for each of these rules?

- **Every** division by 2, 3, 4, 5, 6, 9 and 10 has a remainder.

- **None** of the divisions has a remainder. Why does this happen?

■ For more practice, go to Practice Book 4, page 52.

3G Rounding answers up or down

Discover

Round up or round down?

Solve these divisions, then discuss the answers with a partner.

- Do you need to round the answer up or down? Tick the box.

1 A ferry can carry 9 cars.

   How many ferries are needed
   to carry 116 cars?

   Round up ☐   Round down ☐

2 Yani is packing pineapples into boxes.
   He has 69 pineapples.

   Each box holds 10 pineapples.
   How many boxes does he need?

   Round up ☐   Round down ☐

3 80 laptops are packed into containers.

   Each container holds 6 laptops.

   How many full containers are there?

   Round up ☐   Round down ☐

3G Rounding answers up or down

Work with a partner.

4 Write two division problems where you need to round the answer **up**. Write your problems about:

a people and cars

_____

_____

_____

b your own idea.

_____

_____

_____

I am going to write a problem about some children sharing boxes of cherries.

5 Write two division problems where you need to round the answer **down**. Write your problems about:

a eggs and egg boxes

_____

_____

b your own idea.

_____

_____

_____

Give all your questions to another pair to solve.

 **Stretch zone**

Can you explain why the exact answer is not always important?

■ For more practice, go to Practice Book 4, page 53.

Explore

Sea-view restaurant

Use your notebook, or a piece of paper, for any calculations that you need to do.

1 In this restaurant six people can sit at each table.

How many tables do the staff need to prepare each day?

	Number of people	Number of tables needed
Monday	75	
Tuesday	72	
Wednesday	73	
Thursday	67	
Friday	82	

2 During the holiday season, the restaurant changes the seating so that eight people can sit at each table. How many tables do the staff need to prepare now?

	Number of people	Number of tables needed
Monday	92	
Tuesday	96	
Wednesday	108	
Thursday	115	
Friday	120	

 Stretch zone

Imagine you are the manager of a restaurant. What size tables will you use? Explain your answer.

3 Multiplication and division

59

■ For more practice, go to Practice Book 4, page 54.

Discover

 Multiplication and division

Use the numbers and symbols in the box.

2	3	4	5
6	12	15	18
20	24	30	
÷	×	=	

Key words
- division
- multiplication
- inverse operation

1 Write as many correct multiplication and division sentences as you can.

- You can use the numbers and symbols as many times as you like.

I chose 12, 3 and 4. I wrote these number sentences: 12 ÷ 3 = 4 and 3 × 4 = 12

2 Write five division calculations that have remainder 2.

I know that 2 × 5 = 10, so 12 ÷ 5 will have remainder 2.

Stretch zone

Explain how you used multiplication to help with **question 2.**

Write an easy calculation and a difficult question with remainder 2.

60

3H Multiplication and division as inverse operations

Key words
- division
- multiplication
- inverse operation

Explore

 Multiplication and division facts

Think back

You can use fact families to write different number sentences. For example, I can use the division sentence $21 \div 7 = 3$ to write these other number sentences:

$3 \times 7 = 21$ $\qquad$ $21 \div 3 = 7$ $\qquad$ $7 \times 3 = 21$

Write as many multiplication and division sentences as you can for each start number below.

1 $20 \div \boxed{} = \boxed{}$

3 $54 \div \boxed{} = \boxed{}$

2 $16 \div \boxed{} = \boxed{}$

4 $74 \div \boxed{} = \boxed{}$

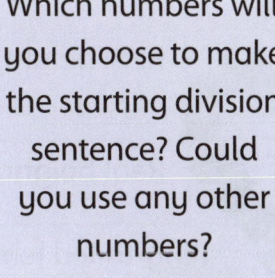

Which numbers will you choose to make the starting division sentence? Could you use any other numbers?

Write the fact family for every starting division sentence that you write.

Stretch zone

Jian says: '$8 \div 2 = 4$ so $2 \div 8 = 4$.' Draw a diagram to explain why Jian is incorrect.

■ For more practice, go to Practice Book 4, page 56.

31 Scaling problems

Discover

Key word
- scale

Animal heights

The animals in these pictures are smaller than in real life.

1   Work out the real height of each animal.

Meerkat

3 cm

Real height is 9 times bigger.

Real height: ☐ cm

Raccoon

3 cm

Real height is 8 times bigger.

Real height: ☐ cm

Camel

2 cm

Real height is 100 times bigger.

Real height: ☐ cm

Ring-tailed lemur

4 cm

Real height is 10 times bigger.

Real height: ☐ cm

Squirrel

3 cm

Real height is 6 times bigger.

Real height: ☐ cm

Giraffe

5 cm

Real height is 100 times bigger.

Real height: ☐ cm

2   Which of these animals is the tallest in real life? _____

3   Which of these animals is the shortest in real life? _____

> **Stretch zone**
>
> In your notebook draw scale drawings of the following animals.
> - A gorilla's real height is 160 cm. Draw the gorilla 20 times smaller.
> - A sloth's real height is 48 cm. Draw the sloth 8 times smaller.

■ For more practice, go to Practice Book 4, page 57.

31 Scaling problems

Explore

Recipes for one person

Key word
- scale

Here are two recipes for butter chicken curry and chocolate ice-cream.

The recipes are for different numbers of people.

- Scale each recipe down so that the amounts are correct for **one** person.

Butter chicken curry for 4 people	Butter chicken curry for 1 person
200 g butter	☐ g butter
1 large onion, chopped	☐ large onion, chopped
4 teaspoons curry powder	☐ teaspoons curry powder
4 chicken breast fillets, cubed	☐ chicken breast fillets, cubed
6 fresh tomatoes, peeled and chopped	☐ fresh tomatoes, peeled and chopped
150 ml tinned tomatoes	☐ ml tinned tomatoes

Chocolate ice-cream for 6 people	Chocolate ice-cream for 1 person
120 g dark chocolate, in pieces	☐ g dark chocolate, in pieces
300 ml milk	☐ ml milk
90 g sugar	☐ g sugar
3 egg yolks	☐ egg yolks
300 ml cream	☐ ml cream

Stretch zone

Scale up the butter chicken recipe so the amounts are correct for 6 people. Write the list of ingredients.

63

■ For more practice, go to Practice Book 4, page 58.

3J Correspondence problems

Discover

Multiplication and division problems

Key words
- proportion
- ratio

1 A box contains 3 tins of tomato soup and 5 tins of mushroom soup.

   a How many tins of tomato soup are there in 3 boxes?

   b How many tins of mushroom soup are there in 5 boxes?

   c I have 27 tins of tomato soup. How many tins of mushroom soup do I have?

   d I need at least 48 tins of mushroom soup. How many boxes do I need?

2 A box contains 4 basketballs and 6 footballs.

To answer **question 1c**, first use division to work out the number of boxes. Then use multiplication to find the answer.

   a How many footballs are there in 5 boxes?

   b How many basketballs are there in 8 boxes?

   c If I have 20 basketballs, how many boxes do I have?

   d I need at least 35 footballs. How many boxes do I need?

Stretch zone

I have 20 more footballs than basketballs. How many boxes do I have?

64

3J Correspondence problems

Explore

Farmyard problem

On my farm there are some chickens and some goats.

I can see 58 legs and 20 heads.

How many chickens and how many goats do I have?

- Show all your workings.

Key words
- proportion
- ratio

There are 20 heads so there must be 20 animals altogether.

Stretch zone

Make up your own problem with two different types of animals. The animals must have different numbers of legs. Give your problem to a friend to solve.

■ For more practice, go to Practice Book 4, page 60.

3 Multiplication and division

Connect

Enclosure problem

A safari park wants to build new enclosures of different shapes for the animals.

I can multiply and divide mentally using times tables facts, doubling and halving, and partitioning and recombining. I can also use written methods such as the grid method or column method.

 Equilateral triangle Square Pentagon Hexagon

 Heptagon Octagon 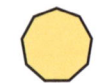 Nonagon Decagon

- Complete the table.

Shape of enclosure	Length of side	Number of sides	Length of fencing required	Cost of fencing ($10 per metre)
Equilateral triangle	87 m			
Square	67 m			
Pentagon	56 m			
Hexagon	49 m			
Heptagon	43 m			
Octagon	36 m			
Nonagon	27 m			
Decagon	19 m			

 **Stretch zone**

The zoo has 108 m of fencing to make one enclosure. What different shapes could the enclosure be, without any fencing left over? The sides can be any length.

3 Multiplication and division

Review

1 Follow the instructions to write three different questions.

a Write a multiplication with a 2-digit number and a 1-digit number, to solve using the grid method.	**b** Write a multiplication with a 3-digit number and a 1-digit number, to solve by partitioning and recombining.	**c** Write a multiplication with three single-digit numbers.

- Give your questions to a partner to answer.

- Mark your partner's answers and correct any errors.

2 Explain how to use doubling to multiply a number by 8.

_____

_____

3 Find at least one 2-digit number to answer each of the following questions.

- Show all your workings.

a Find a 2-digit number that divides exactly by 2, 3, 4, 6, 8 and 12.

b Find a 2-digit number that divides by 2 with remainder 1, by 5 with remainder 2 and by 6 with remainder 3.

c Find a 2-digit number that divides by 4 with remainder 3, by 5 with remainder 3 and by 6 with remainder 3.

4 Fractions and decimals

In this unit you will:

- recognise families of equivalent fractions
- recall decimal equivalents of some fractions
- count on and back in hundredths
- add and subtract fractions
- understand the effect of dividing by 10 and 100
- round decimals to the nearest whole number
- solve problems involving fractions and decimals, including money problems.

?

When do we use fractions and when do we use decimals in everyday life? Why do we need both?

When we measure or use money, do we use fractions or decimals?

Engage

When we divide into groups, do we use decimals or fractions?

When we share food, do we use fractions or decimals?

Which fractions and decimals do you know?

4A Recognising fractions

Key words
- fraction pair
- numerator
- denominator

Discover

Fraction pairs to 1

> **Worked example**
>
> In this bar model you can see a whole divided into five equal parts.
>
> | | | | | |
> |---|---|---|---|---|
>
> Each part is $\frac{1}{5}$ of the whole.
>
> The shaded red part is $\frac{1}{5}$ of the whole.
>
> The unshaded white part is $\frac{4}{5}$ of the whole.

Draw a bar model to show each fraction. Then write the fraction that is unshaded.

1   The shaded part is $\frac{1}{4}$ of the whole.
    What fraction is unshaded?

2   The shaded part is $\frac{7}{8}$ of the whole.
    What fraction is unshaded?

3   The shaded part is $\frac{5}{10}$ of the whole.
    What fraction is unshaded?

4   The shaded part is $\frac{1}{3}$ of the whole.
    What fraction is unshaded?

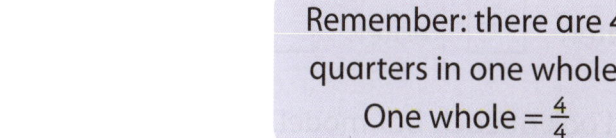

Remember: there are 4 quarters in one whole.
One whole $= \frac{4}{4}$

Stretch zone

Explain to a partner the strategy you used to find the unshaded fraction.
Draw some more examples to show that your strategy works every time.

4 Fractions and decimals

■ For more practice, go to Practice Book 4, page 62.

4A Recognising fractions

Explore 1

Key words
- fraction pairs
- numerator
- denominator

Fraction sums to 1

1 What fraction of each pizza has been eaten?

What fraction has not been eaten? The first one is done for you.

| Eaten $\frac{4}{6}$ | Eaten ☐ | Eaten ☐ | Eaten ☐ |
| Not eaten $\frac{2}{6}$ | Not eaten ☐ | Not eaten ☐ | Not eaten ☐ |

For the last pizza, you choose how much has been eaten and not eaten.

2 Look at each bar model. Complete the fraction sum.
One is done for you

a

$\frac{1}{3} + \boxed{\frac{1}{3} + \frac{1}{3}} = \boxed{\frac{3}{3}} = \boxed{1}$

I added together all the sections of the bar model.

b

$\frac{1}{4} + \boxed{} = \boxed{\frac{4}{4}} = \boxed{1}$

c

$\frac{1}{8} + \boxed{} = \boxed{} = \boxed{}$

d

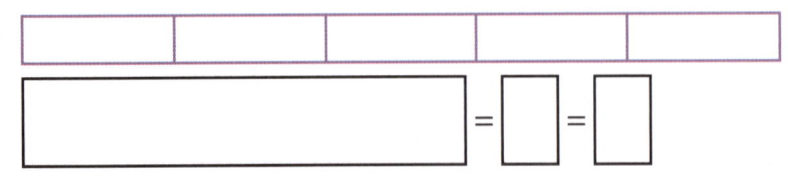

$\boxed{} = \boxed{} = \boxed{}$

Stretch zone

Divide a rectangle into any number of equal pieces. Write the fraction sum for your bar model.

■ For more practice, go to Practice Book 4, page 63.

Explore 2

Patterns in multiplication tables

I Use the lines to help you divide the square into equal shapes, to match the fraction. The first one is done for you.

a Divide into thirds. $\frac{3}{3}$

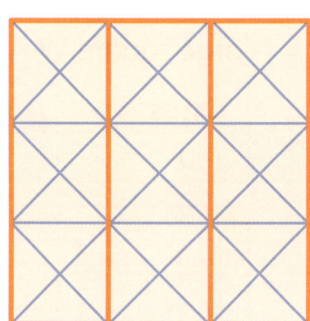

I drew rectangles to divide the first square into thirds. There are $\frac{3}{3}$.

b Divide into sixths. $\frac{6}{6}$

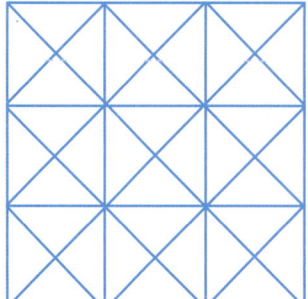

c Divide into ninths. $\frac{9}{9}$

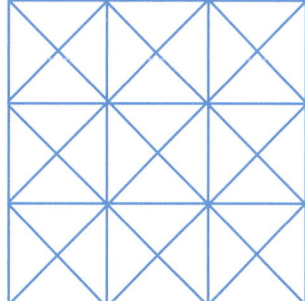

Is there more than one way to divide the square each time?

2 Use different colours to show ways of dividing the square into quarters.

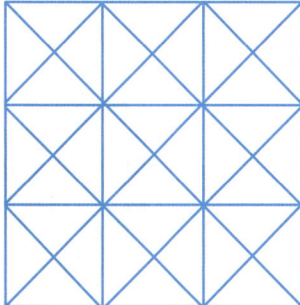
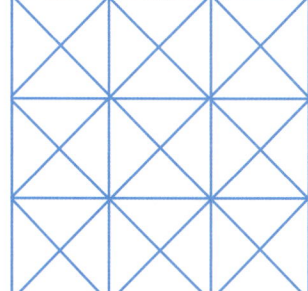
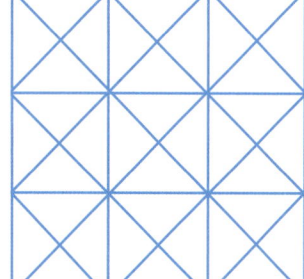
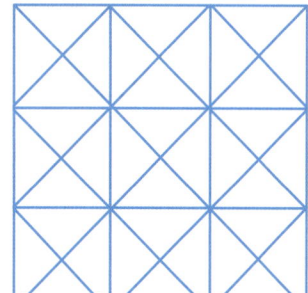

Stretch zone

Can you divide the same square into any other fractions? Does adding more lines help you to do this?

4 Fractions and decimals

■ For more practice, go to Practice Book 4, page 64.

4B Hundredths

Key words
- tenths
- hundredths
- decimal
- decimal fraction
- decimal point

Discover

Introducing hundredths

Think back

This square is divided into 100 smaller squares. One column is coloured. This is a tenth of the square. We write $\frac{1}{10}$ or 0.1

One small square is a hundredth of the large square. We write $\frac{1}{100}$ or 0.01

Ones	.	Tenths	Hundredths
0	.	0	1

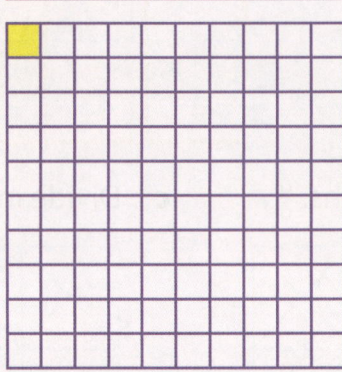

Colour squares on these 100-squares.

- How much of the square have you coloured? Write the fraction and the decimal fraction.

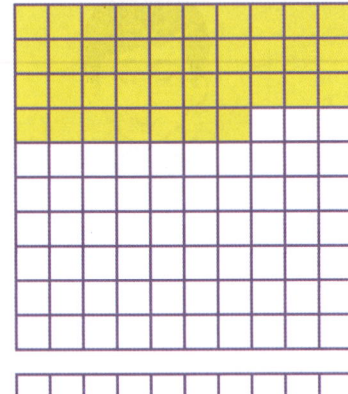

I coloured ⬚ 37 ⬚ squares.

This is ⬚ $\frac{37}{100}$ ⬚ or ⬚ 0.37 ⬚

The first one is done for you.

I coloured ⬚ squares.

This is ⬚ or ⬚

Discover (continued)

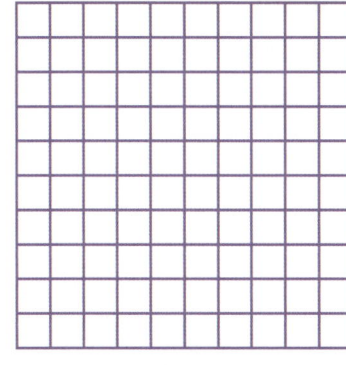

I coloured ☐ squares.

This is ☐ or ☐

You can choose any numbers between 1 and 100.

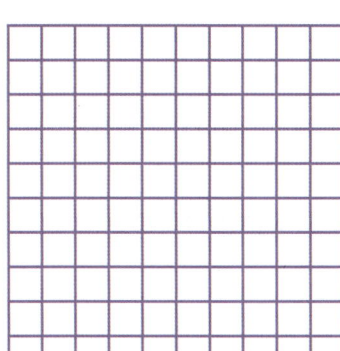

I coloured ☐ squares.

This is ☐ or ☐

I coloured ☐ squares.

This is ☐ or ☐

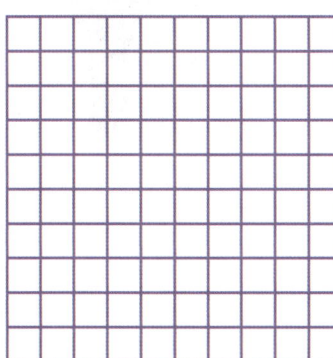

I coloured ☐ squares.

This is ☐ or ☐

Colour between 60 and 80 squares on this last 100-square.

4 Fractions and decimals

Stretch zone

If I colour one quarter of the square, what decimal fraction is this? What decimal fraction is three quarters of the square?

■ For more practice, go to Practice Book 4, page 65.

4B Hundredths

Count in hundredths

Key words
- tenths
- hundredths
- decimals

Think back

This number sequence counts on in tenths.
0.5 0.6 0.7 0.8 0.9 1.0 1.1 1.2

We can count on and back in hundredths.

1 Write the next numbers in these sequences.

a 0.15 0.16 0.17 0.18 ☐ ☐

b 1.38 1.37 1.36 1.35 ☐ ☐

c 0.96 0.97 0.98 0.99 ☐ ☐

d 1.65 1.64 1.63 1.62 ☐ ☐

I counted on in hundredths from 1.52:

1.52 1.53 1.54 1.56 1.57 …

2 Write the next numbers in these sequences.

a $\frac{22}{100}$ $\frac{23}{100}$ $\frac{24}{100}$ $\frac{25}{100}$ ☐ ☐

b $\frac{52}{100}$ $\frac{53}{100}$ $\frac{54}{100}$ $\frac{55}{100}$ ☐ ☐

c $\frac{99}{100}$ $\frac{98}{100}$ $\frac{97}{100}$ $\frac{96}{100}$ ☐ ☐

What is the same and what is different about counting in tenths and counting in hundredths?

3 Write the missing numbers in these sequences.

a 4.98 ☐ 5.00 5.01 ☐ ☐

b 3.42 3.43 ☐ ☐ 3.46

c 6.42 6.41 ☐ 6.39 ☐ 6.37

Stretch zone

Zahid says that 2.65 is halfway between 2.6 and 2.7. Is he correct? Explain how you know.

74

4C Equivalent fractions

Discover

Equivalent cube patterns

Key words
- equivalent fractions
- fraction wall
- simplify

Think back

Remember: $\frac{3}{4} + \frac{1}{4} = 1$

1 Use some cubes to make a shape that is $\frac{3}{4}$ one colour and $\frac{1}{4}$ another colour.

- Sketch your shape and write the number of cubes.

- Repeat two more times with different numbers of cubes.

Sketch 1	Sketch 2	Sketch 3

Number of cubes: ☐   Number of cubes: ☐   Number of cubes: ☐

2 Can you make a $\frac{3}{4}$, $\frac{1}{4}$ pattern with 10 cubes? Yes / No

3 What do you notice about the numbers that you have used to make your shapes?

Discover (continued)

Think back

This grid shows part of the multiplication tables for 1 and 4.

×1	1	2	3	4	5	6
×4	4	8	12	16	20	24

When the numbers are positioned like this, they look like fractions.
Can you see the pattern in the numbers?

4   Follow the instructions to colour the diagrams.

Colour 1 part out of 4.	Colour 2 parts out of 8.	Colour 3 parts out of 12.	Colour 4 parts out of 16.	Colour 5 parts out of 20.	Colour 6 parts out of 24.

- What do you notice about the fraction you have coloured in each diagram?

  _____

- Write five fractions that are equivalent to $\frac{1}{4}$.

5   Complete this table.

×1	1	2	3	4	5	6
×3	3					

- Write three fractions that are equivalent to $\frac{1}{3}$.

Stretch zone

Write a rule for finding equivalent fractions.

■ For more practice, go to Practice Book 4, page 67.

4C Equivalent fractions

Explore

Spot equivalent fractions

Key words

- equivalent fractions
- fraction wall
- simplify

1 Can you make a $\frac{3}{4}$, $\frac{1}{4}$ pattern with the following? Circle yes or no.

a 24 red cubes and 8 yellow cubes Yes / No

b 30 blue cubes and 10 pink cubes Yes / No

c 19 green cubes and 7 red cubes Yes / No

d 120 white cubes and 40 yellow cubes Yes / No

When I divide a number of cubes into quarters, each part needs to divide by 4.

2 Write two more examples of $\frac{3}{4}$, $\frac{1}{4}$ cube patterns that you can make.

____

____

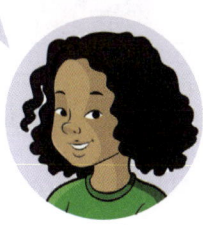

- Draw your cube patterns.

Explore (continued)

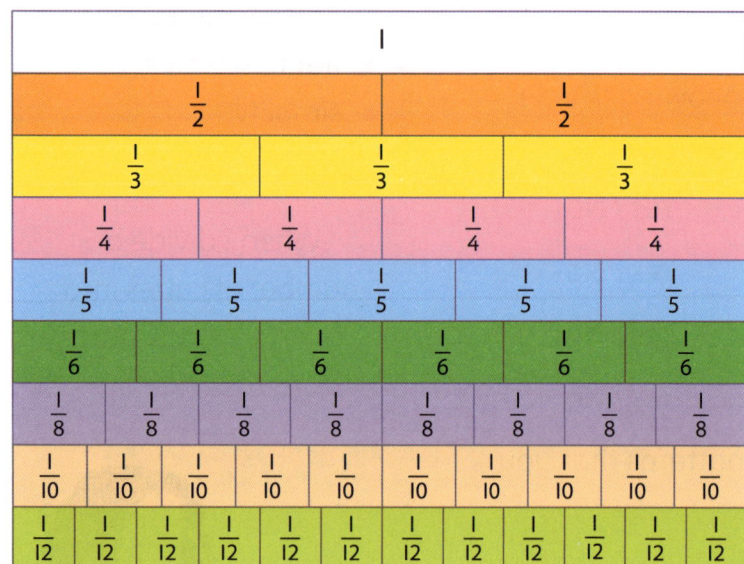

3 Use the fraction wall to find an equivalent fraction for:

a $\frac{2}{3}$

b $\frac{3}{4}$

c $\frac{1}{2}$

d $\frac{1}{3}$

e $\frac{1}{5}$

f $\frac{2}{5}$

g $\frac{4}{12}$

h $\frac{6}{10}$

Can you find more than one equivalent fraction for some of these fractions?

4 Are these pairs of fractions equivalent? Tick Yes or No.

			Yes	No
a	$\frac{3}{4}$	$\frac{5}{8}$	☐	☐
b	$\frac{3}{5}$	$\frac{6}{10}$	☐	☐
c	$\frac{6}{12}$	$\frac{2}{4}$	☐	☐
d	$\frac{7}{8}$	$\frac{8}{10}$	☐	☐

Stretch zone

Write three equivalent fractions for $\frac{3}{5}$. How will you work out the fractions that are not on the fraction wall?

■ For more practice, go to Practice Book 4, page 68.

4D Using equivalence to order fractions

Discover

Order fractions

> **Think back**
>
> If a fraction is equal to $\frac{1}{2}$, the denominator is double the numerator.
>
> $\frac{2}{4}, \frac{3}{6}, \frac{15}{30}, \frac{23}{46}$ are all equal to $\frac{1}{2}$.

I Write at least six fractions in each column of this table.

Less than $\frac{1}{2}$	Greater than $\frac{1}{2}$

How do you know your fractions are in the correct column?

2 What fractions does this fraction wall show? Discuss with a partner then label the fractions.

3 Find six different fractions on the fraction wall and write them in order below.

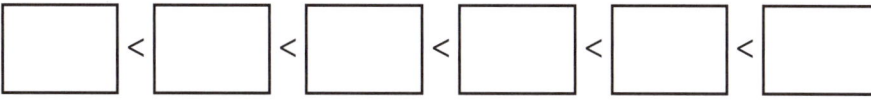

Remember that < means less than.

Stretch zone

Write some fractions between $\frac{1}{2}$ and $\frac{3}{4}$. Write your fractions in order.

■ For more practice, go to Practice Book 4, page 69.

Explore

Equivalent fraction clues

Key words
- equivalent
- numerator
- denominator

I Work with a partner. Use the clues to work out these fractions.

a This fraction is equal to $\frac{1}{4}$. The denominator is 8.

The fraction is: ☐

b This fraction is equal to $\frac{1}{2}$. The numerator and denominator have a total of 12.

The fraction is: ☐

c The numerator in this fraction is 2 less than the denominator. The fraction is equal to $\frac{3}{4}$.

The fraction is: ☐

d The numerator and denominator are both odd numbers and have a total of 6.

The fraction is: ☐

The fraction I am thinking of is equal to $\frac{1}{2}$. The denominator is 10.

I think your fraction is $\frac{5}{10}$.

2 Draw a diagram to show each fraction below. Then draw a diagram to show one fraction that is less than the fraction and one fraction that is greater than the fraction.

a $\frac{7}{10}$

b $\frac{5}{8}$

Stretch zone

Complete this ordered list of fractions. $\frac{1}{2} <$ 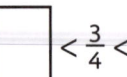 $< \frac{3}{4} <$ $< \frac{9}{10}$

■ For more practice, go to Practice Book 4, page 70.

Discover

Unit fractions and non-unit fractions of quantities

Think back

A unit fraction has I as the numerator.
$\frac{1}{2}$, $\frac{1}{8}$, $\frac{1}{15}$ are all unit fractions.

To find $\frac{1}{4}$ of a number, you divide by 4.

To find $\frac{1}{10}$ of a number, you divide by 10.

I Look at this fraction spider diagram.

- What other unit fractions can you add to this diagram that gives a whole number answer?

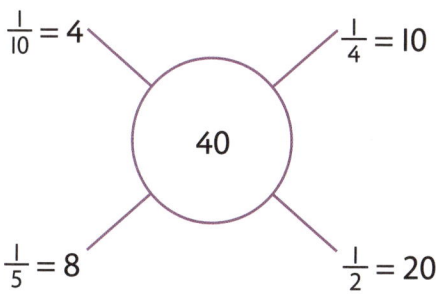

$\frac{1}{10} = 4$ $\frac{1}{4} = 10$

40

$\frac{1}{5} = 8$ $\frac{1}{2} = 20$

2 Choose two of these numbers: 30, 20, 24, 50.

- Draw a fraction spider diagram for each number below.

Include all the unit fractions that give a whole number answer.

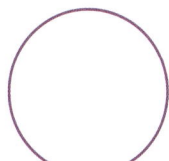

Discover (continued)

Worked example

How do you find $\frac{3}{4}$ of 20?

First find $\frac{1}{4}$ of 20 by dividing by 4. $\qquad \frac{1}{4}$ of 20 = 5

Then multiply by 3 to find $\frac{3}{4}$. $\qquad \frac{3}{4}$ of 20 = 3 × 5 = 15

I drew a diagram to show this calculation.

3 Find $\frac{3}{4}$ of each number.

• Draw a diagram to show each calculation.

a $\frac{3}{4}$ of 12 = ⬜

b $\frac{3}{4}$ of 20 = ⬜

c $\frac{3}{4}$ of 28 = ⬜

4 Find $\frac{2}{3}$ of each number.

• Draw a diagram to show each calculation.

a $\frac{2}{3}$ of 15 = ⬜

b $\frac{2}{3}$ of 24 = ⬜

c $\frac{2}{3}$ of 66 = ⬜

Stretch zone

Write instructions to find $\frac{5}{8}$ of a number: First … Then …

■ For more practice, go to Practice Book 4, page 71.

4E Finding fractions of quantities

Key words
- fraction
- division
- divisor

Fractions of amounts

1 Work out the value of the fraction of each number.

a $\frac{2}{3}$ of 39 $\frac{1}{3}$ of 39 = ☐   so $\frac{2}{3}$ of 39 = ☐

b $\frac{3}{4}$ of 40 $\frac{1}{4}$ of 40 = ☐   so $\frac{3}{4}$ of 40 = ☐

c $\frac{2}{3}$ of 69 $\frac{1}{3}$ of 69 = ☐   so $\frac{2}{3}$ of 69 = ☐

d $\frac{2}{3}$ of 33 $\frac{1}{3}$ of 33 = ☐   so $\frac{2}{3}$ of 33 = ☐

e $\frac{2}{5}$ of 45 $\frac{1}{5}$ of 45 = ☐   so $\frac{2}{5}$ of 45 = ☐

f $\frac{3}{8}$ of 32 $\frac{1}{8}$ of 32 = ☐   so $\frac{3}{8}$ of 32 = ☐

g $\frac{2}{7}$ of 14 $\frac{1}{7}$ of 14 = ☐   so $\frac{2}{7}$ of 14 = ☐

h $\frac{5}{6}$ of 42 $\frac{1}{6}$ of 42 = ☐   so $\frac{5}{6}$ of 42 = ☐

To find $\frac{2}{3}$ of 30, I first worked out $\frac{1}{3}$ of 30. $\frac{1}{3}$ is 10, so $\frac{2}{3}$ of 30 is 20.

2 Write <, > or = to make each statement correct.

a $\frac{1}{2}$ of 90 ☐ $\frac{2}{3}$ of 39

b $\frac{3}{4}$ of 40 ☐ $\frac{1}{2}$ of 58

c $\frac{2}{3}$ of 69 ☐ $\frac{3}{4}$ of 80

d $\frac{1}{2}$ of 38 ☐ $\frac{2}{3}$ of 33

e $\frac{2}{3}$ of 72 ☐ $\frac{3}{4}$ of 64

f $\frac{3}{5}$ of 70 ☐ $\frac{5}{7}$ of 63

First work out the answer to each side of the statement, then write the correct symbol to make the statement correct.

4 Fractions and decimals

4E Finding fractions of quantities

Explore (continued)

Use your notebook for your workings.

Solve these word problems.

3 The book I am reading is 256 pages long. Tonight I read as far as page 96.

a How many pages more than $\frac{1}{4}$ of the book have I read?

b How many more pages do I have to read until I have read $\frac{1}{2}$ of the book?

c What do you notice about your two answers? Explain why this happens?

_____

_____

4 My grandmother has $270 to share between her three grandchildren. She gives $\frac{1}{2}$ of the money to the eldest; $\frac{1}{3}$ to the middle grandchild and the rest to the youngest.

a How much does the youngest grandchild receive?

$ ☐

b What fraction of the money is this?

5 You are saving up to buy a bicycle. The bicycle costs $159 but you want to have $\frac{1}{4}$ of your savings left after you have bought the bicycle. How much do you need to save before you buy the bicycle?

Use this bar model to help you.

$159	

I need to save $ ☐

Stretch zone

Mason says that $\frac{1}{2}$ is always greater than $\frac{1}{4}$. Is he correct?

■ For more practice, go to Practice Book 4, page 72.

4F Adding and subtracting fractions

Discover

Key words
- fraction
- addition
- subtraction

Use bar models to add and subtract

Think back

When you add fractions with the same denominator, just add the numerators.

$\frac{1}{5} + \frac{2}{5} = \frac{3}{5}$

Do subtraction in a similar way.

$\frac{3}{5} - \frac{2}{5} = \frac{1}{5}$

We can draw bar models to show addition and subtraction of fractions.

Worked example

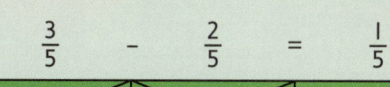

$\frac{1}{5}$ + $\frac{2}{5}$ = $\frac{3}{5}$

$\frac{3}{5}$ − $\frac{2}{5}$ = $\frac{1}{5}$

Can you see how the addition bar model shows the calculation? Use a different colour to show the fraction that you add.

Can you see how the subtraction bar model shows the calculation? Cross out the fraction that you subtract.

Draw a similar bar model to show each calculation below.

1 $\frac{7}{8} - \frac{5}{8} = \boxed{}$

2 $\frac{3}{6} + \frac{1}{6} = \boxed{}$

3 $\frac{9}{10} - \frac{7}{10} = \boxed{}$

4 $\frac{1}{5} + \frac{3}{5} = \boxed{}$

5 $\frac{6}{7} + \frac{1}{7} = \boxed{}$

Stretch zone

Write an easy calculation and a difficult calculation with the answer $\frac{1}{2}$.

4 Fractions and decimals

85

■ For more practice, go to Practice Book 4, page 73.

Explore

If that is the answer, what is the question?

Write a calculation with the answer given.

- Then draw a bar model to show each calculation.

1   ▢ □ ▢ $= \frac{2}{5}$

2   ▢ □ ▢ $= \frac{3}{5}$

3   ▢ □ ▢ $= \frac{5}{6}$

4   ▢ □ ▢ $= \frac{1}{8}$

5   ▢ □ ▢ $= \frac{7}{10}$

6   ▢ □ ▢ $= \frac{5}{7}$

Key words
- unit fraction
- equivalent fraction
- addition
- subtraction

Use a mixture of addition and subtraction calculations.

Stretch zone

Write an easy calculation and a difficult calculation with the answer $\frac{5}{8}$.

■ For more practice, go to Practice Book 4, page 74.

4G Equivalent fractions and decimals

Discover 1

Equivalent tenths

Think back

In a decimal fraction the decimal point separates the whole number part from the fraction part.

The first place after the point is for tenths.

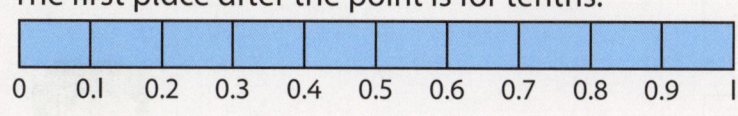

| 0 | 0.1 | 0.2 | 0.3 | 0.4 | 0.5 | 0.6 | 0.7 | 0.8 | 0.9 | 1 |

Key words
- tenths
- decimal point
- one decimal place

1 What part of each diagram is shaded?

- Write a fraction and a decimal fraction.

a 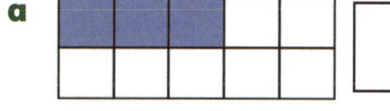 $\frac{3}{10}$ | 0.3

b

c

d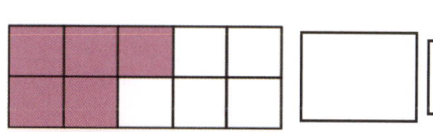

e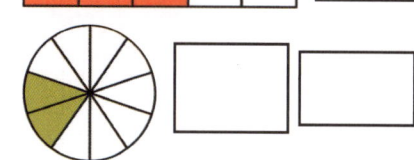

f

2 Write each group of numbers in order, from smallest to largest.

a $\frac{1}{2}$, 0.3, seven tenths

b four and three tenths, 4.5, $3\frac{9}{10}$

3 What number is each arrow pointing to on the number line?

- Write the numbers in decimal form. One is done for you.

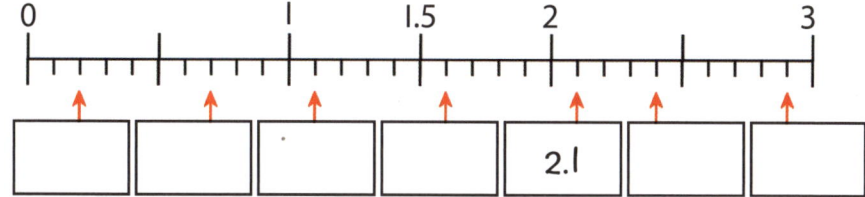

| 0 | 1 | 1.5 | 2 | 3 |

| | | | | 2.1 | | |

Count the divisions between the whole numbers. So how much is each division worth?

Stretch zone

Explain how you know if a decimal fraction is greater than 1.

87

■ For more practice, go to Practice Book 4, page 75.

Discover 2

Fraction and decimal games

Key words
- tenths
- decimal point
- one decimal place

1 Match each **decimal equivalent** with the correct fraction.

- One is done for you.

Fraction   **Decimal equivalent**

Fraction	Decimal equivalent
$\frac{1}{100}$	0.5
$\frac{1}{4}$	0.4
$\frac{1}{5}$	0.75
$\frac{3}{10}$	0.01
$\frac{3}{4}$	0.9
$\frac{2}{5}$	0.25
$\frac{1}{2}$	0.3
$\frac{9}{10}$	0.2
$\frac{6}{10}$	0.1
$\frac{1}{10}$	0.6

Try to learn the matching pairs.

2 Label all the fractions and decimals from **question 1** on the number line.

Write the fractions above the line and the decimals below the line.

0   1

Discover 2 (continued)

3 Play this game with a partner.

- Write a fraction in the 'Fraction' column of each of the **first** three rows.

- Write a decimal fraction in the 'Decimal' column of each of the **last** three rows.

- Swap your table with a partner. Complete their table.

Include some easy fractions and decimals and some difficult ones!

Fraction		Decimal
	=	
	=	
	=	
	=	
	=	
	=	

Stretch zone

Write an explanation of how to find a decimal equivalent of a fraction.

■ For more practice, go to Practice Book 4, page 76.

4G Equivalent fractions and decimals

Explore

Write and draw equivalents

Colour the 100-squares below to show the equivalent decimal fractions. The first one is done for you.

Key words
- tenths
- decimal point
- one decimal place

a $\frac{20}{100} = \boxed{\frac{2}{10}} = \boxed{0.2}$

1	2	3	4	5	6	7	8	9	10
11	12	13	14	15	16	17	18	19	20
21	22	23	24	25	26	27	28	29	30
31	32	33	34	35	36	37	38	39	40
41	42	43	44	45	46	47	48	49	50
51	52	53	54	55	56	57	58	59	60
61	62	63	64	65	66	67	68	69	70
71	72	73	74	75	76	77	78	79	80
81	82	83	84	85	86	87	88	89	90
91	92	93	94	95	96	97	98	99	100

d $\frac{3}{4} = \boxed{} = \boxed{}$

1	2	3	4	5	6	7	8	9	10
11	12	13	14	15	16	17	18	19	20
21	22	23	24	25	26	27	28	29	30
31	32	33	34	35	36	37	38	39	40
41	42	43	44	45	46	47	48	49	50
51	52	53	54	55	56	57	58	59	60
61	62	63	64	65	66	67	68	69	70
71	72	73	74	75	76	77	78	79	80
81	82	83	84	85	86	87	88	89	90
91	92	93	94	95	96	97	98	99	100

For $\frac{20}{100}$, I coloured 20 squares. $\frac{20}{100}$ is equivalent to $\frac{2}{10}$ and 0.2

b $\frac{1}{4} = \boxed{} = \boxed{}$

1	2	3	4	5	6	7	8	9	10
11	12	13	14	15	16	17	18	19	20
21	22	23	24	25	26	27	28	29	30
31	32	33	34	35	36	37	38	39	40
41	42	43	44	45	46	47	48	49	50
51	52	53	54	55	56	57	58	59	60
61	62	63	64	65	66	67	68	69	70
71	72	73	74	75	76	77	78	79	80
81	82	83	84	85	86	87	88	89	90
91	92	93	94	95	96	97	98	99	100

e $\frac{3}{10} = \boxed{} = \boxed{}$

1	2	3	4	5	6	7	8	9	10
11	12	13	14	15	16	17	18	19	20
21	22	23	24	25	26	27	28	29	30
31	32	33	34	35	36	37	38	39	40
41	42	43	44	45	46	47	48	49	50
51	52	53	54	55	56	57	58	59	60
61	62	63	64	65	66	67	68	69	70
71	72	73	74	75	76	77	78	79	80
81	82	83	84	85	86	87	88	89	90
91	92	93	94	95	96	97	98	99	100

c $\frac{1}{2} = \boxed{} = \boxed{}$

1	2	3	4	5	6	7	8	9	10
11	12	13	14	15	16	17	18	19	20
21	22	23	24	25	26	27	28	29	30
31	32	33	34	35	36	37	38	39	40
41	42	43	44	45	46	47	48	49	50
51	52	53	54	55	56	57	58	59	60
61	62	63	64	65	66	67	68	69	70
71	72	73	74	75	76	77	78	79	80
81	82	83	84	85	86	87	88	89	90
91	92	93	94	95	96	97	98	99	100

f $\frac{7}{100} = \boxed{}$

1	2	3	4	5	6	7	8	9	10
11	12	13	14	15	16	17	18	19	20
21	22	23	24	25	26	27	28	29	30
31	32	33	34	35	36	37	38	39	40
41	42	43	44	45	46	47	48	49	50
51	52	53	54	55	56	57	58	59	60
61	62	63	64	65	66	67	68	69	70
71	72	73	74	75	76	77	78	79	80
81	82	83	84	85	86	87	88	89	90
91	92	93	94	95	96	97	98	99	100

90

Explore (continued)

2 Complete this table.

Words	Decimal	Fraction	Number line
one tenth			
	0.2		
		$\frac{3}{10}$	
six tenths			
	0.7		
		$\frac{8}{10}$	
ten tenths	1.0	1	

Stretch zone

Can you find an equivalent fraction for all of the fractions in the table?
For example, $\frac{8}{10} = \frac{4}{5}$.

■ For more practice, go to Practice Book 4, page 77.

Key words
- ones
- tenths
- hundredths

Discover

Divide by 10 on a place-value grid

Think back

When you multiply a number by 10, the digits move one place to the left in the place-value grid.

	Hundreds	Tens	Ones	·	Tenths	Hundredths
52.6		5	2	·	6	0
52.6 × 10	5	2	6	·	0	0

52.6 × 10 = 526
What do you think happens when you divide by 10?

Complete the place-value grids.

1

	Hundreds	Tens	Ones	·	Tenths	Hundredths
115				·		
115 ÷ 10				·		

2

	Hundreds	Tens	Ones	·	Tenths	Hundredths
215				·		
215 ÷ 10				·		

3

	Hundreds	Tens	Ones	·	Tenths	Hundredths
21.5				·		
21.5 ÷ 10				·		

4

	Hundreds	Tens	Ones	·	Tenths	Hundredths
15				·		
15 ÷ 10				·		

Check your answers using a calculator. What happens to the digits in the numbers?

5 Complete these division calculations.

a 115 ÷ 100 = ⬚

c 21.5 ÷ 100 = ⬚

b 215 ÷ 100 = ⬚

d 15 ÷ 100 = ⬚

Explain the rule for dividing by 10 or 100 to a partner.

Stretch zone

What is the same and what is different about multiplying and dividing by 10 and 100.

4H Dividing by 10 and 100

Multiply and divide by 10 and 100

Think back

When we **multiply** by 10 each digit becomes 10 times bigger. The ones become tens. The tens become hundreds. The hundreds become thousands.

For example: $456 \times 10 = 4560$

When we **divide** by 10 each digit becomes 10 times smaller. The thousands become hundreds. The hundreds become tens. The tens become ones.

For example: $1570 \div 10 = 157$

1 Complete these multiplication calculations.

a $234 \times 10 =$

b $23.4 \times 10 =$

c $2.34 \times 10 =$

d $2.34 \times 100 =$

e $9.62 \times 10 =$

f $9.62 \times 100 =$

g $96.2 \times 10 =$

h $962 \times 10 =$

2 Complete these division calculations.

a $340 \div 10 =$

b $340 \div 100 =$

c $34 \div 10 =$

d $34 \div 100 =$

e $25 \div 10 =$

f $25 \div 100 =$

g $89 \div 10 =$

h $89 \div 100 =$

Stretch zone

Talk to a partner. Each of you complete one of these sentences.

When we divide by 100 the tens become …

When we divide by 100 the ones become …

■ For more practice, go to Practice Book 4, page 79.

41 Rounding to the nearest whole number

Discover

Key words
- rounding
- nearest whole number
- tenths
- hundredths

Round on a number line

Label the ends of each number line.

- Mark each decimal number on the number line.

- Round each decimal number to the nearest whole number. The first one is done for you.

1 3.8 rounded to the nearest whole number is [4].

> A whole number has no fraction or decimal parts.

2 8.8 rounded to the nearest whole number is [   ].

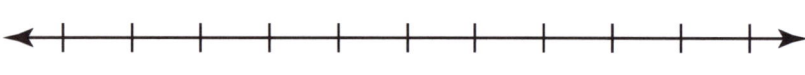

3 4.4 rounded to the nearest whole number is [   ].

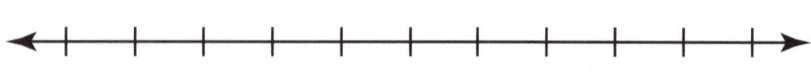

> 3.8 is between 3 and 4 but it is nearer to 4.

4 8.6 rounded to the nearest whole number is [   ].

5 25.5 rounded to the nearest whole number is [   ].

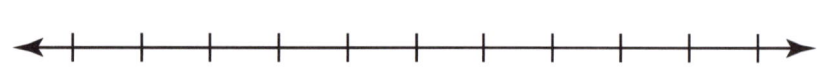

> If a number is halfway between two numbers, we round up to the next whole number.

Stretch zone

Amina is thinking of a number. She rounds it to the nearest whole number and the answer is 17. What number might Amina be thinking of? Write at least four possible numbers.

94

■ For more practice, go to Practice Book 4, page 80.

41 Rounding to the nearest whole number

Explore

Round to the nearest whole, ten or hundred

Key words
- rounding
- nearest whole number
- tenths
- hundredths

Use the number lines to help you round each number.

1 337 rounded to the nearest 10 is [ ].

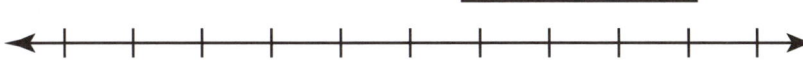

2 337 rounded to the nearest 100 is [ ].

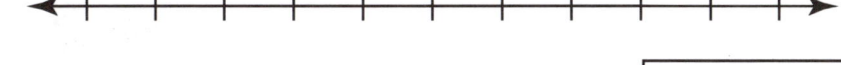

3 33.7 rounded to the nearest whole number is [ ].

Read the questions very carefully. What is the start number and what are you rounding it to?

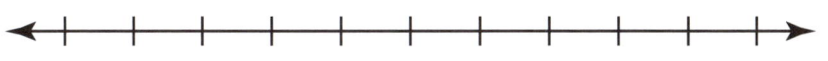

4 3.7 rounded to the nearest whole number is [ ].

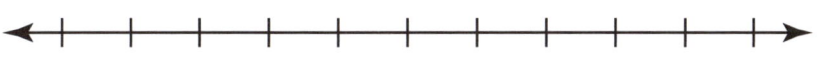

5 3.3 rounded to the nearest whole number is [ ].

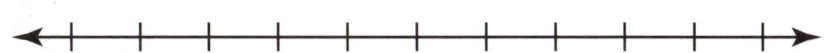

6 16.5 rounded to the nearest whole number is [ ].

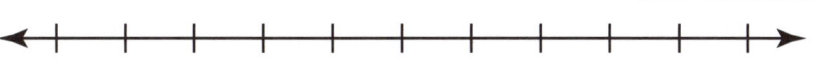

7 99.9 rounded to the nearest whole number is [ ].

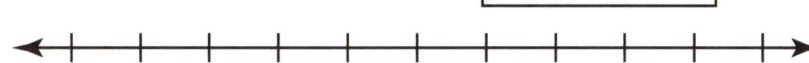

8 99.9 rounded to the nearest 10 is [ ].

Stretch zone

If I round a number to the nearest whole number and then to the nearest 10, the two answers will always be different. True or false?

4 Fractions and decimals

■ For more practice, go to Practice Book 4, page 81.

Discover

Greater or smaller decimals

Worked example

Which is bigger, 1.53 or 1.72?

We can draw a diagram, using a 100-square, to find out.

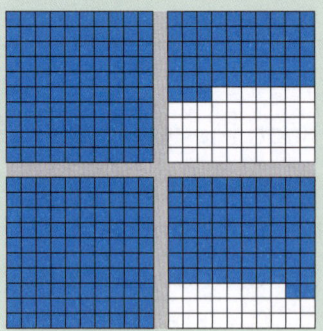

There are more squares shaded for 1.72 so 1.72 is the bigger number.

We write: 1.72 > 1.53

Remember: > means 'is greater than' and < means 'is less than'.

1   Use the digits 4, 5, 6 to make six different numbers with two places of decimals.

You can use each digit more than once.

- Write your numbers here.

2   Complete these statements using your numbers.

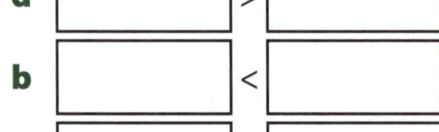

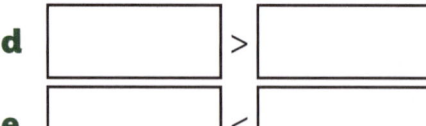

a   [ ] > [ ]   d   [ ] > [ ]

b   [ ] < [ ]   e   [ ] < [ ]

c   [ ] > [ ]   f   [ ] > [ ] > [ ]

Stretch zone

Jakub says that 1.56 is greater than 2.05 because 56 is greater than 5.

Is he correct? Explain your answer.

■ For more practice, go to Practice Book 4, page 82.

Explore

Order and compare decimals

Key words
- places of decimals
- tenths
- hundredths

1 Look at the numbers in the middle column of the table.

- Write a number greater than and a number less than each number.

An example is shown in the table.

Less than	Number	Greater than
2.45	2.55	3.12
	3.85	
	1.85	
	0.5	
	10.5	
	25.12	
	0.12	
	1.2	

2 Use the digits 2, 4 and 6 to make four different numbers with two places of decimals. Write them in order.

◻ < ◻ < ◻ < ◻

3 Use two or more of the digits 0, 2, 4 and 6 to complete each row of this place-value grid.

	Thousands	Hundreds	Tens	Ones	·	Tenths	Hundredths
The largest number					·		
The smallest number					·		
A number less than 5					·		
A number greater than $\frac{1}{2}$					·		

 Stretch zone

Write three numbers between 1.5 and 1.75

4 Fractions and decimals

97

Discover

Decimals in money

Think back

When we use decimals to write amounts of money, we **always** include two digits after the decimal point. We sometimes have to write a zero in the hundredths place. For example, we write $2.30, not $2.3

Key words

- dollar
- cents
- tenths
- hundredths

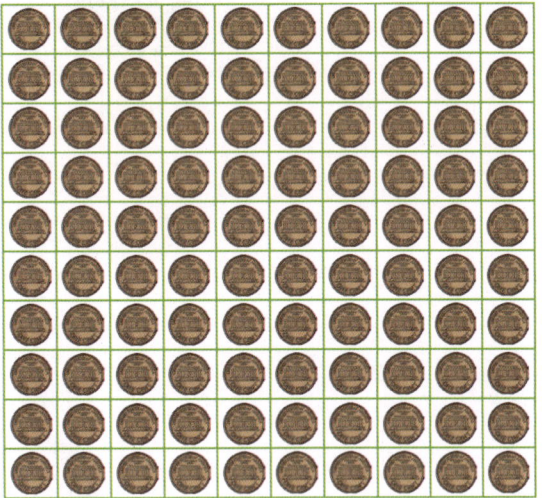

I know there are 100 cents in $1 so there are 50 cents in $\frac{1}{2}$ a dollar. I write this as $0.50.

Use the '100-cents square' to help you complete the table.

1 Write each fraction of a dollar as a number of cents and then as a decimal amount.

Fraction of $1	Number of cents	Decimal amount
$\frac{1}{2}$	50 ¢	$0.50
$\frac{1}{10}$		
$\frac{1}{4}$		
$\frac{1}{5}$		
$\frac{3}{4}$		
$\frac{3}{10}$		
$\frac{3}{5}$		
$\frac{1}{100}$		

Discover (continued)

2   You have a bag of money containing dollar notes ($1),
quarters (25¢) and 1 cent coins (1¢).

> There are a lot of
> possible answers!

- You can only take a total of five coins and notes out
of the bag.

- What different amounts can you make?

Stretch zone

What is the smallest possible amount? What is the largest possible amount?

■ For more practice, go to Practice Book 4, page 84.

Explore

Decimals in money and measures

1¢

5¢

10¢

25¢

In the USA, a 25¢ coin is called a quarter, a 10¢ coin is called a dime, a 5¢ coin is called a nickel and a 1¢ coin is called a penny.

1 How much money is there in each purse?

- Write your answer in dollars, using decimals.

I can see that there is $1.26 in the first purse.

a $1.26 — 1c 25c ONE DOLLAR

d ____ — 1c 25c 10c ONE DOLLAR

g ____ — 5c 1c 1c 1c 1c ONE DOLLAR

b ____ — 10c 25c 1c 1c 25c ONE ... ONE DOLLAR

e ____ — 25c 25c 25c 5c ONE ONE DOLLAR

h ____ — 25c 10c 5c ONE ONE DOLLAR

c ____ — 25c 25c 1c 1c 1c ONE ONE DOLLAR

f ____ — 5c ONE ONE DOLLAR

i ____ — 10c 1c 25c 25c 25c 25c 25c 25c

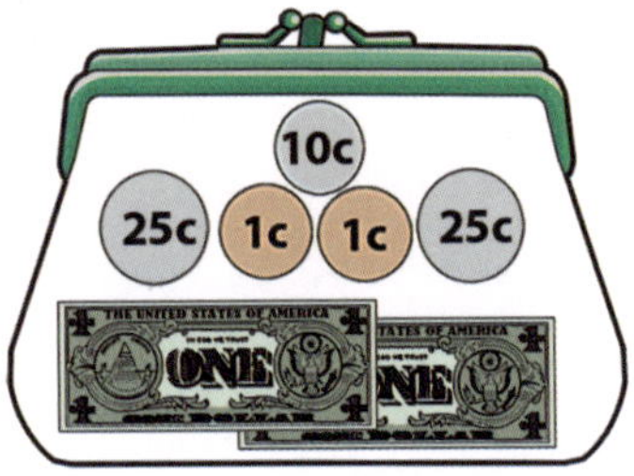

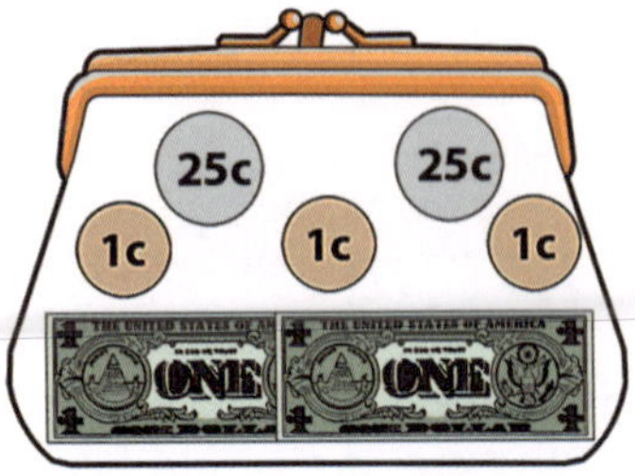

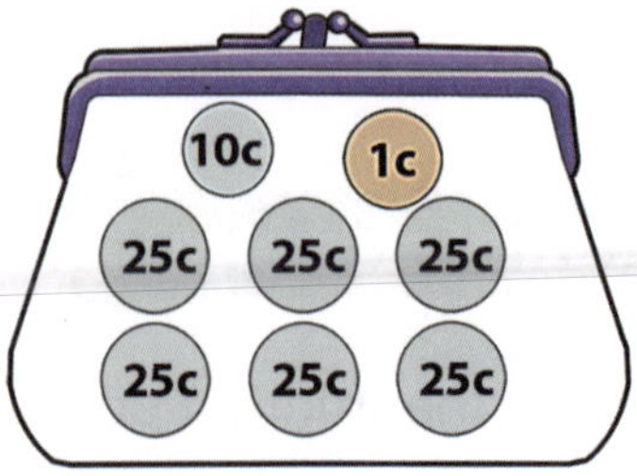

Explore (continued)

Think back

There are 100 centimetres in 1 metre. So 1 cm is $\frac{1}{100}$ of 1 m.

I converted 125 cm to metres. It is 1.25 m.

2 Convert these distances from centimetres to metres.

a 178 cm ⟶ ☐ m

b 300 cm ⟶ ☐ m

c 432 cm ⟶ ☐ m

d 10 cm ⟶ ☐ m

e 4 cm ⟶ ☐ m

f 50 cm ⟶ ☐ m

When we use decimals for measuring we write 1.2 m, not 1.20 m.

3 Measure these lines. Write the lengths in millimetres and centimetres. The first one is done for you.

		Length (mm)	Length (cm)
a	____	12 mm	1.2 cm
b	_____		
c	_____		
d	_____		
e	_____		
f	____		
g	_____		

Stretch zone

Write a measurement very close to, but just shorter than 2 m. Write a measurement very close to, but just longer than 2 m.

■ For more practice, go to Practice Book 4, page 85.

Connect

Pizza restaurant fractions and decimals

I know when to use fractions and when to use decimals. I can use both and convert between them.

The students in your class decide to go to a pizza restaurant for a meal together.

The number of students in my class is ☐.

1 How many pizzas do you need so that everyone can have:

   a $\frac{1}{4}$ pizza each? ☐

   b $\frac{1}{3}$ pizza each? ☐

   c $\frac{1}{2}$ pizza each? ☐

2 All the students want a 0.25 litre milkshake.

   How many litres of milkshake do you need so that everyone can have a milkshake? ☐

3 The restaurant sells chocolate cake.

   a How many whole cakes do you need to buy so that everyone can have $\frac{1}{8}$ of a cake each? ☐

   b Is there any cake left over? Yes / No

   c If yes, how much is left over?  of a cake.

Stretch zone

Write two questions of your own about the pizza restaurant that involve fractions or decimals. Give them to a partner to solve.

4 Fractions and decimals

Review

1 Draw a diagram that shows $\frac{3}{4}$.

You could draw a circle, a rectangle, or something else. How many parts does your diagram need?

2 Write an addition or subtraction calculation with $\frac{3}{4}$ in the question.

_____

3 Write an addition or subtraction calculation with $\frac{3}{4}$ as the answer.

_____

4 Write a measures problem with the answer $\frac{3}{4}$, written as a decimal.

_____

_____

You could use metres, litres, kilograms or units of your choice.

5 Draw a diagram that shows $\frac{5}{8}$.

6 Write an addition or subtraction calculation with $\frac{5}{8}$ in the question.

_____

7 Write an addition or subtraction calculation with $\frac{5}{8}$ as the answer.

_____

8 Write a measures problem with the answer $\frac{5}{8}$, written as a decimal.

_____

_____

5 Length, mass and capacity

Why do we need to measure things? How do we measure things?

In this unit you will:

- estimate, compare and calculate different measures, including money
- convert between different units of measure.

Engage

How long was the longest baseball hit ever?

What else do we measure?

When do we measure?

How much water does a watering can hold?

What units do we use to measure things?

What are the heaviest vegetables?

5A Estimating, measuring and recording length

Discover

Measure length

 I Measure the height of each person in your group. Draw a table of the measurements. Record all the heights in centimetres (cm), and in metres (m) and centimetres.

Name	Height in cm	Height in m and cm
Zara	132	1.32
Rashid	127	1.27

2 Think of a way to measure the length of your step as accurately as possible. Check your choice with your teacher.

Add another column to your table and write the step length of everyone in your group.

3 Work with a partner.

a Choose a long distance to measure. For example, you could choose the length of a football pitch or the length of the school hall.

b Measure the distance in steps.

The _____ is ☐ steps long.

c Use a calculator to convert the length to metres.

☐ m

d Measure the length again using a trundle wheel or metre stick. ☐ m

e Are your answers in **c** and **d** the same? Yes / No

Stretch zone

Estimate the length of your classroom, in metres. Use your knowledge of your step length to help you.

Key words
- kilometre
- metre
- centimetre
- millimetre

Use a metre stick or a tape measure.

Remember to write a column header!

Why might your answers to **c** and **d** be different?

5 Length, mass and capacity

■ For more practice, go to Practice Book 4, page 87.

5A Estimating, measuring and recording length

Explore 1

Units of length

1 Draw lines to match each length to the best unit of measure. One is done for you.

Length of an ant	
Length of a football pitch	millimetres (mm)
Height of a door	
Distance across America	centimetres (cm)
Length of a book	
Height of a tree	metres (m)
Length of a banana	
Length of an orange pip	kilometres (km)

I know that a banana is about 20 cm long.

Remember:
1 km = 1000 m.

2 Convert the units.

a 2 km = ⬚ m

b 1.5 km = ⬚ m

c ⬚ km = 7300 m

d ⬚ km = 3400 m

e 9.1 km = ⬚ m

f 5.6 km = ⬚ m

 **Stretch zone**

Explain how to convert kilometres to centimetres.

■ For more practice, go to Practice Book 4, page 88.

5A Estimating, measuring and recording length

Explore 2

Estimate length

Key words
- kilometre
- metre
- centimetre
- millimetre

1   Look in your classroom for some objects that are between $\frac{1}{2}$ metre (50 cm) and 1 metre long.

- **Estimate** the length of each object. Record your estimate in the table.

- Measure each object to the nearest centimetre. Record the actual length in the table.

Object	Estimated length	Actual length

2   Circle the correct measurement for each object.

The height of a door	The length of a pencil	The height of an elephant	The length of your finger
Approximately:	Approximately:	Approximately:	Approximately:
4 m	18 mm	50 cm	60 mm
200 cm	20 m	3 m	10 cm
100 cm	18 cm	50 m	6 mm

Stretch zone

Estimate the height of your classroom. Explain how you made the estimate. How can you measure the height to check your estimate?

5 Length, mass and capacity

107

■ For more practice, go to Practice Book 4, page 89.

Discover

Estimate and measure mass

Key words
- mass
- kilogram
- gram

1 Choose six classroom objects.

I chose a book and a pencil case as my first two objects.

- Hold two of the objects, one in each hand, to compare their masses.
- Estimate the order of all six objects from lightest to heaviest.
- Write the names of the objects, in order, in the table.

Lightest to heaviest	Object	Estimate (grams)	Actual mass (grams)
1			
2			
3			
4			
5			
6			

A bag of sugar has a mass of 1 kg. Does this help with your estimates?

It is not easy to estimate mass! Continue to practise and you will improve.

2 Estimate the mass of each object in grams. Record your estimates in the second column of the table.

3 Now use some balance scales to measure the actual mass of each item.

- Did you write the objects in the correct order?

5B Estimating, measuring and recording mass

Discover (continued)

4 Choose six different objects from the classroom that you think have a mass less than a kilogram.

- Hold a 1 kg weight in one hand and an object in your other hand. Estimate the mass of each object, in grams.

I think my mathematics book has a mass less than 1 kg.

5 Write your estimates in the table.

6 Now use electronic scales to weigh each object. Record the actual mass in the table.

Did your estimating improve each time? Why?

Object	Estimate (grams)	Actual mass (grams)

5 Length, mass and capacity

Stretch zone

Which do you think is heavier: a small container full of sand or an identical container full of water? Test your prediction.

■ For more practice, go to Practice Book 4, page 90.

Explore

Mass problems

1 Solve these problems. Show your workings.

   a A coin has a mass of 23 g.

     What is the mass of 8 coins?

I will work out 8×20 and 8×3 to find the answer.

	g

   b A crate of apples has a mass of 5.25 kg.

     The mass of the empty crate is 485 g.

     What is the mass of the apples?

	g

   c A cake has a mass of 960 g.

     You cut it into 12 equal slices.

     What is the mass of each slice?

	g

5B Estimating, measuring and recording mass

Explore (continued)

2 This table shows the masses of some different fruits.

Lemon	Orange	Apple	Pineapple	Banana	Melon	Lime	Mango
110 g	300 g	160 g	890 g	170 g	1000 g	90 g	260 g

a Which fruits have a mass less than $\frac{1}{4}$ kg?

_____

b Which fruits have a mass greater than $\frac{1}{2}$ kg?

_____

c Which fruits have a mass between $\frac{1}{4}$ kg and $\frac{1}{2}$ kg?

_____

d Which two fruits have a total mass of 1 kg?

_____

e Which two fruits have a total mass that is the same
   as the mass of the mango?

_____

f Which three fruits have a total mass of $\frac{1}{2}$ kg?

_____

3 Complete the labels on this scale to show both grams and kilograms.

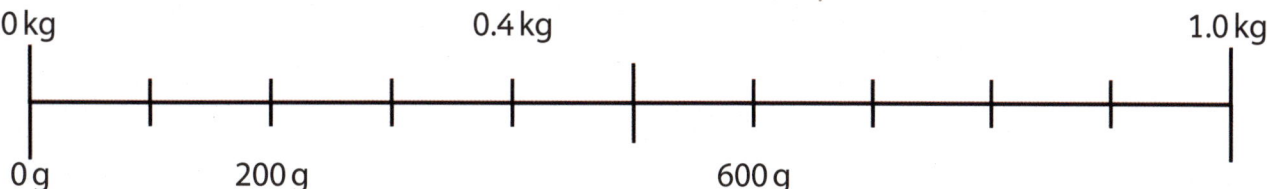

0 kg   0.4 kg   1.0 kg

0 g   200 g   600 g

Stretch zone

Write your own word problem with the answer 500 g.

■ For more practice, go to Practice Book 4, page 91.

Discover

Capacity experiments

Try these two experiments.

1 Find a large container that can hold water.

- Estimate the level of I litre of water in the container.

- Draw an arrow on a sticky note and stick it onto the container to show your estimate.

- Check your estimate by pouring in I litre of water.

- Move the sticky note to the correct level.

- Estimate the level of 2 litres and use another sticky note to mark your estimate.

- Repeat until you reach the top of the container.

2 Fill a measuring cylinder to about half full.

- Record the water level in the table below.

- Lower a stone into the measuring cylinder, using string or wire.

  You will see that the water level rises.

- Complete the table.

Level of water at start	
New level when stone added	
Difference	

Are you getting better at estimating capacity? It takes practice!

The difference in the water level is equal to the amount of space the stone takes up. Archimedes discovered this more than 2000 years ago!

Stretch zone

Repeat **question 2** with a different stone or another object. Use your results in the table to help you estimate what the difference will be.

■ For more practice, go to Practice Book 4, page 92.

Explore

Record capacity

Think back

I litre = 1 000 ml, so $\frac{1}{2}$ litre = 500 ml

1 Circle the larger measurement in each pair. Two are done for you.

$\frac{1}{2}$ litre	(550 ml)	350 ml	$\frac{1}{4}$ litre	$\frac{3}{4}$ litre	700 ml	450 ml	($\frac{1}{2}$ litre)
I litre	850 ml	$\frac{1}{4}$ litre	140 ml	I litre	1100 ml	$\frac{3}{4}$ litre	850 ml

2 These bottles all hold 1 litre. How much do you need to add to each bottle to fill it? The first one is done for you.

a	**b**	**c**	**d**	**e**	**f**	**g**	**h**
370 ml	260 ml	450 ml	610 ml	890 ml	730 ml	120 ml	580 ml
630 ml							

3 Complete the table by converting the capacities.

	Capacity (ml)	Capacity (litres)
Carton of apple juice		0.4 litre
Bottle of olive oil	800 ml	
Bottle of lemonade	1100 ml	
Carton of orange juice		1.2 litres
Carton of milk	2000 ml	
Large bottle of water		3.5 litres

Stretch zone

How can you quickly convert millilitres to litres and from litres to millilitres? Does this method work with all units of measure?

5 Length, mass and capacity

113

■ For more practice, go to Practice Book 4, page 93.

5D Using and reading scales

Discover 1

Read different scales

Try these two experiments. Work in a group.

> This is a spring balance or newton meter.

1 Use the grams scale on a spring balance.

- Estimate the mass of a pencil case.
- Now use the spring balance to measure the mass.
- Repeat with other pencil cases.

Whose pencil case?	Estimate (grams)	Actual mass (grams)

Key words
- kilo-
- milli-

You use a spring balance in science lessons. It measures force in newtons or mass in grams.

Look carefully at the scale to read the measurement accurately.

2 Mix different amounts of red and yellow water together. Use a measuring cylinder to measure the amounts. What do you notice about the different mixtures?

Number of parts red to yellow water	Amount of red to make 100 ml total	Amount of yellow to make 100 ml total	Colour of mixture
I red, I yellow			
2 red, 3 yellow			
3 red, 2 yellow	60 ml	40 ml	
I red, 3 yellow			

Stretch zone

What do you think the colours of the mixtures will be if you use red and blue, or yellow and blue?

■ For more practice, go to Practice Book 4, page 94.

Discover 2

Use a ruler

Key words
- kilo-
- milli-

Think back

We measure very small lengths in millimetres.

Remember: 10 mm = 1 cm

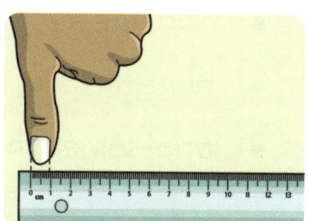

1 Use your ruler to measure some small objects.

- Record their lengths in the table. One is done for you.
- Choose two more objects to add to the table.

Object	Length in millimetres	Length in centimetres
Width of a pencil	6 mm	0.6 cm
Width of your thumbnail		
Thickness of your textbook		

Why do you think it is quite difficult to measure **to the nearest millimetre**?

2 Measure these lines as accurately as you can.

a —— Length: ⬚ mm

b ——— Length: ⬚ mm

c — Length: ⬚ mm

3 Draw these lines as accurately as you can.

a 12 mm

b 7 mm

c 5 mm

Use a sharp pencil to draw the lines.

Stretch zone

Can you think of something that is approximately 1 mm thick? Can you think of something that is approximately 5 mm thick?

5 Length, mass and capacity

115

■ For more practice, go to Practice Book 4, page 95.

Explore

Scales for length, mass and capacity

1 Look at each scale.

- Write the number that each arrow is pointing to.

- Write the difference between the two arrows.

- Write something that you can use the scale to measure.

Worked example

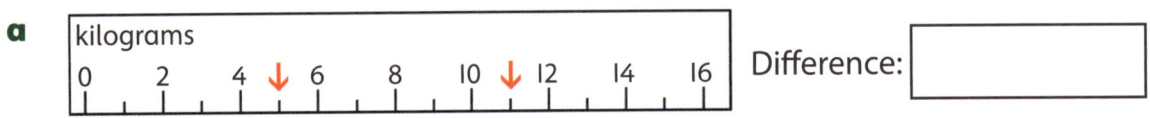

centimetres

Difference: | 30 cm

I can use this scale to measure ___the length of a book.___

a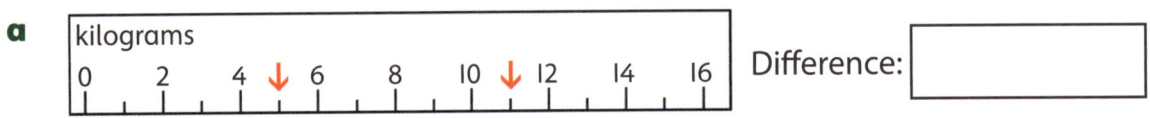

kilograms

Difference: [   ]

I can use this scale to measure _____

b

metres

Difference: [   ]

I can use this scale to measure _____

c

millilitres

Difference: [   ]

I can use this scale to measure _____

d

grams

Difference: [   ]

I can use this scale to measure _____

e

litres

Difference: [   ]

I can use this scale to measure _____

5D Using and reading scales

2 Draw a line to match each parcel to the correct scales.

 $1\frac{3}{4}$ kg

 $1\frac{1}{2}$ kg

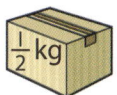 $\frac{1}{2}$ kg

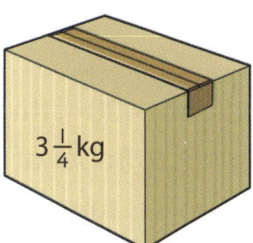 $3\frac{1}{4}$ kg

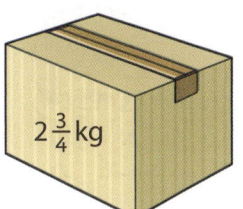 $2\frac{3}{4}$ kg

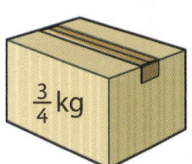 $\frac{3}{4}$ kg

 $1\frac{1}{4}$ kg

 $\frac{1}{4}$ kg

a

b

c

d

e

f

g

h

5 Length, mass and capacity

Explore (continued)

3 You have these metric weights:

1 × 1 kg	1 × 50 g
1 × 500 g	2 × 20 g
2 × 200 g	1 × 10 g
1 × 100 g	1 × 5 g

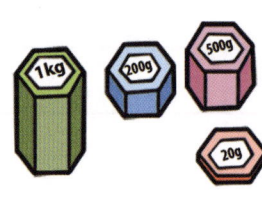

- Use the smallest number of weights to balance each mass.

- Write the weights that you use as an addition sentence.

Worked example

$420 g = \underline{200 g + 200 g + 20 g}$

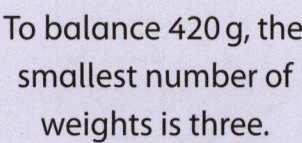

To balance 420 g, the smallest number of weights is three.

a $1\frac{1}{4}$ kg = _____

b 810 g = _____

c $\frac{3}{4}$ kg = _____

d 145 g = _____

e 160 g = _____

f 1 kg 480 g = _____

g 2 kg 45 g = _____

h 985 g = _____

Stretch zone

Use 1 g, 2 g, 5 g and 10 g weights to make every mass between 1 g and 20 g. Use as few weights as possible. For example: 4 g = 2 g + 2 g.

■ For more practice, go to Practice Book 4, page 96.

5 Length, mass and capacity

Connect

Animal fact cards

1 Research six animals and complete the animal facts.

Animal: Mass: Length: Speed:	Animal: Mass: Length: Speed:
Animal: Mass: Length: Speed:	Animal: Mass: Length: Speed:
Animal: Mass: Length: Speed:	Animal: Mass: Length: Speed:

> We need to measure things in everyday life. Sometimes we can estimate measurements and sometimes we need to measure accurately.

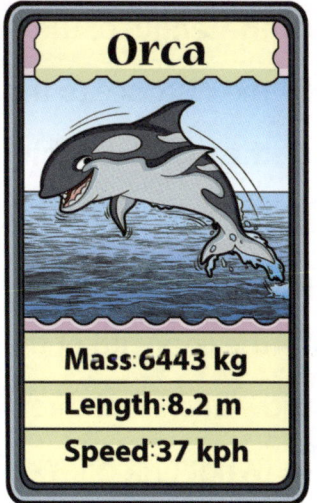

Orca

Mass: 6443 kg
Length: 8.2 m
Speed: 37 kph

2 Use your facts to answer these questions.

a Which is the heaviest animal? _____

b Which is the lightest? _____

c Which is the fastest animal? _____

d Which is the slowest? _____

e Which is the longest animal? _____

f Which is the shortest? _____

> You could use your facts to create some fact cards of your own.

Stretch zone

Is it true that the heavier an animal is, the slower it is?

5 Length, mass and capacity

Review

1 Write the meaning of each prefix.

   a kilo- _____

   b centi- _____

   c milli- _____

2 Write the correct unit to measure:

   a the length of the classroom _____

   b the distance to the moon _____

   c the mass of a coin _____

   d the mass of a human _____

   e the capacity of a cup _____

   f the capacity of the petrol tank in a car. _____

3 Draw and label three different measuring tools that have a scale.

   • What unit does each scale use?

   • Write one object that you can measure using each measuring tool.

Unit: _____	Unit: _____	Unit: _____
Used to measure:	Used to measure:	Used to measure:
_____	_____	_____

4 Luc weighs 75.6 kg. He picks up a suitcase that weighs 8.2 kg. What is the total mass of Luc and his suitcase?

   [___] kg

6 Area and perimeter

? How do we calculate area and perimeter? What units do we use?

In this unit you will:

- measure and calculate the perimeter of a shape in centimetres and metres
- find the area of shapes by counting squares.

Engage

How much bigger is your teacher's desk than your desk?

What is the area of your book cover? What is the perimeter?

What about your desk?

How many books will fit onto your desk?

Discover

Investigate area and perimeter

Key words
- area
- perimeter
- square centimetres (cm²)

I On centimetre-squared paper, draw five different rectangles, each with a **perimeter** of 20 cm.

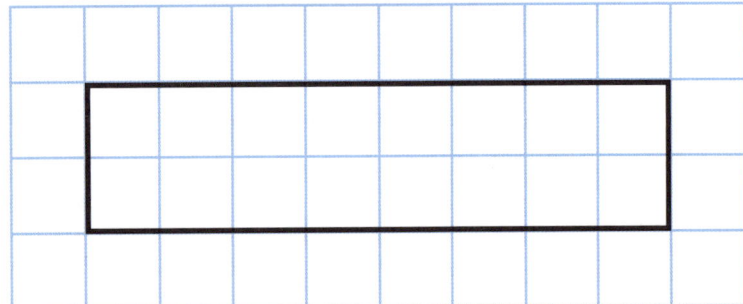

My rectangle is 2 cm wide and 8 cm long. The perimeter is 20 cm and the area is $2 \times 8 = 16$ cm².

2 Count the squares to work out the area of each rectangle. Complete this table. One is done for you.

Length	Width	Area (cm²)	Perimeter (cm)
8	2	16	20
			20
			20
			20
			20

3 On centimetre-squared paper, draw six different rectangles with an **area** of 24 cm². Complete this table.

Length	Width	Area (cm²)	Perimeter (cm)
		24	
		24	
		24	
		24	
		24	

Stretch zone

Look at the rectangle with the largest perimeter in **question 3**. Does a rectangle with this width always have the largest perimeter? Try it out with some rectangles of different areas.

■ For more practice, go to Practice Book 4, page 98.

Calculate perimeters

Key words
- area
- perimeter
- square centimetres (cm²)

I   Measure the side lengths of each rectangle and calculate the perimeter.

a

Perimeter: ☐ cm

b

Perimeter: ☐ cm

c

Perimeter: ☐ cm

d

Perimeter: ☐ cm

Remember to line up your ruler so that 0 is at the start of the side you are measuring.

2   A rug maker wants to add ribbon around the edges of his rugs. The ribbon costs $6 per metre. How much does it cost to add ribbon around the edge of each rug? Complete the table.

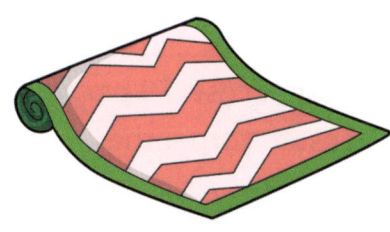

Length of rug (m)	Width (m)	Perimeter (m)	Cost of ribbon ($)
3	5		
4	5		
5	5		
6	5		
4	4		
4	6		
6	3		

Stretch zone

What is the difference between the cost of the ribbon for a 6 m × 5 m rug and the cost of the ribbon for two 3 m × 5 m rugs?

6 Area and perimeter

123

■ For more practice, go to Practice Book 4, page 99.

Explore 2

Calculate area

In the grids below, each square represents 1 m × 1 m.

1 Floor tiles cost $25 per square metre. How much does it cost to tile these rooms? Draw a floor plan for each room.

a Room A is 5 m long and 3 m wide.

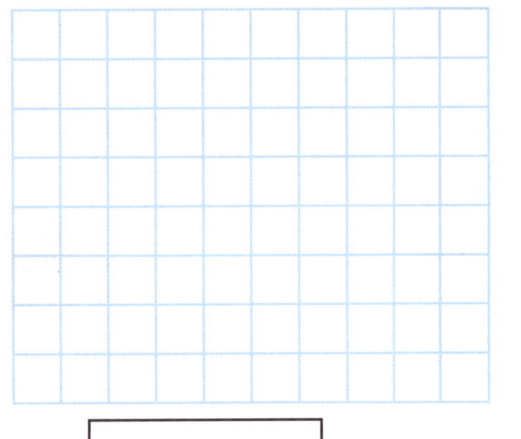

Cost:

b Room B is 4 m square.

Cost:

2 Carpet costs $9 per **square metre**. How much does it cost to carpet these rooms? Draw a floor plan for each room.

a Room C is 4 m long and 2.5 m wide.

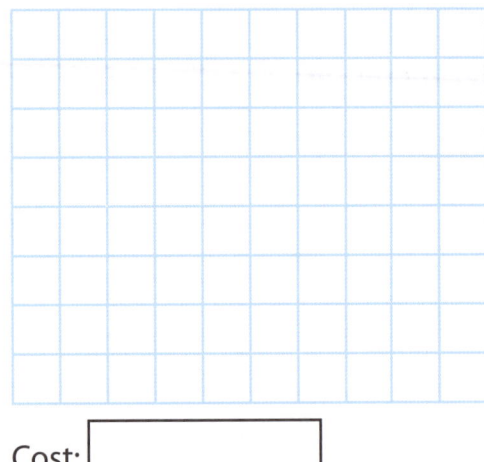

Cost:

b Room D is 8 m long and 6.5 m wide

Cost:

Stretch zone

You decide to use floor tiles instead of carpet for the rooms in **question 2**.
How much does it cost to tile each room?

■ For more practice, go to Practice Book 4, page 100.

6B Finding the area of rectilinear shapes

Discover

Estimate and calculate area and perimeter

You are going to estimate and then measure the perimeter and area of your classroom.

Key words
- area
- perimeter
- square metres (m²)
- dimensions

1 Estimate the length and width of your classroom.

- Calculate the estimated perimeter of your classroom.
- Calculate the estimated area of your classroom.
- Record your estimates in the table.

	Estimate	Measurement
Length		
Width		
Perimeter (m)		
Area (m²)		

2 Measure the actual length and width of your classroom to the nearest metre.

- Calculate the perimeter and area of your classroom.
- Record your measurements in the table.

 **3** Choose one of these areas: 30 cm² 36 cm² 40 cm² 48 cm²

For your chosen area, calculate the length and width of the rectangle that has:

- the smallest perimeter

  length [   ] cm × width [   ] cm

- the largest perimeter

  length [   ] cm × width [   ] cm

I chose 36 cm².
My rectangle could be
1 cm × 36 cm,
2 cm × 18 cm,
3 cm × 12 cm ...

Stretch zone

Test your answers by drawing all the possible rectangles for your chosen area on squared paper, and then calculating the perimeters.

■ For more practice, go to Practice Book 4, page 101.

Explore 1

Patterns in area and perimeter

Complete the tables. Explore the areas and perimeters of the rectangles in the tables. The first row of each table is done for you.

Key words

- area
- perimeter
- square metres (m²)
- dimensions

1

Length × width	Perimeter	Area
1 cm × 1 cm	4 cm	1 cm²
1 cm × 2 cm		
1 cm × 3 cm		
1 cm × 4 cm		
1 cm ×		

You could draw all the rectangles on centimetre-squared paper.

2

Length × width	Perimeter	Area
2 cm × 1 cm	6 cm	2 cm²
2 cm × 2 cm		
2 cm × 3 cm		
2 cm × 4 cm		
2 cm ×		

Can you see any patterns in the perimeters and areas? What do you notice?

Stretch zone

In another set of rectangles, the length is 3 cm and the width increases by 1 cm each time. Can you predict the patterns in the perimeters and areas?

■ For more practice, go to Practice Book 4, page 102.

Explore 2

Draw shapes with the same area

Key words
- area
- perimeter
- square metres (m²)
- dimensions

I Find the area, in squares, of each shape. Then draw a different shape with the same area.

My shapes

a

The area is ☐ squares.

b

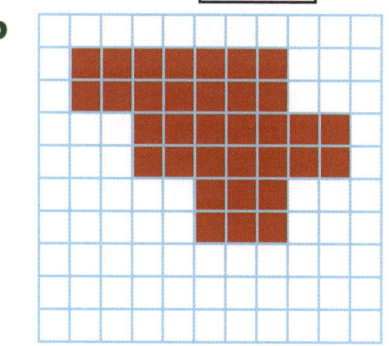

The area is ☐ squares.

c

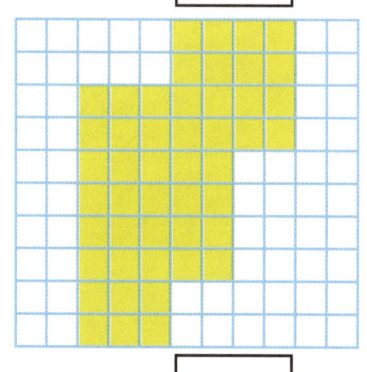

The area is ☐ squares.

Is there a quicker way to find the area, rather than counting all the squares?

 Stretch zone

Calculate the difference between the perimeter of each of your shapes and the perimeter of the original shape.

6 Area and perimeter

127

■ For more practice, go to Practice Book 4, page 103.

6 Area and perimeter

Connect

Design a stable

Hana has a large area of land. She wants to build a stable for her horse on part of her land. She wants the stable to be a rectangular shape with a perimeter of 50 m.

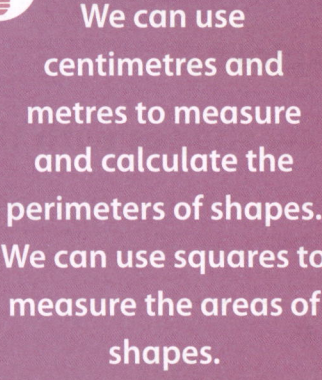

> We can use centimetres and metres to measure and calculate the perimeters of shapes. We can use squares to measure the areas of shapes.

1 Work in a group. What are some possible areas for Hana's stable?

2 On paper, sketch some designs using your areas. For example:

5 m | Area = 100 m² |
20 m

> Label the dimensions on your sketches. But you do not need to draw the designs to scale.

- Remember to label the area on each design.

- Check your drawings to make sure the perimeters are correct.

3 Hana wants the largest possible area for her stable. Which of your designs is the best for Hana to use? Explain why.

The best design for Hana to use is _____

because _____

_____

 Stretch zone

Draw a scale diagram of your best design. Use I cm in your drawing to represent 2 m in real life.

6 Area and perimeter

Review

1 Draw four different rectangles in the centimetre-squared grid below. All the rectangles must have a perimeter of 30 cm.

- Label each rectangle with its dimensions.
- Write the area in the centre of each rectangle.

2 I want to tile the floor of a room that measures 5 m × 3 m. Tiles cost $2.50 per square metre. How much will it cost to tile the room?

7 Time

Why do we measure time?
How do we measure time?

In this unit you will:

- read and write analogue and digital 12- and 24-hour clock times

- solve problems involving converting from hours to minutes, minutes to seconds, years to months, and weeks to days.

Engage

At what time of day do you think this photo was taken?

What units of time do you know?

When do you need to tell the time?

When do you need to know how long something takes?

7A Different ways of telling the time

Discover

Convert times

Key words
- hour
- minute
- analogue clock
- digital clock

1 Complete the table. Use 24-hour clock times for the digital clocks.

Time in words	Digital	Analogue
I get up at		
I have breakfast at		
I arrive at school at		
School finishes at		
I arrive home at		
I eat at		
I go to bed at		

I get up at quarter past 7 in the morning. The digital time is 07:15.

To convert to 24-hour clock time, we add 12 to the hours after midday. So 3 p.m. is 15:00.

2 At what time did you finish **question 1**? Write the time to the nearest minute in words, as a 24-hour clock digital time and using a.m. or p.m.

_____

_____

Discover (continued)

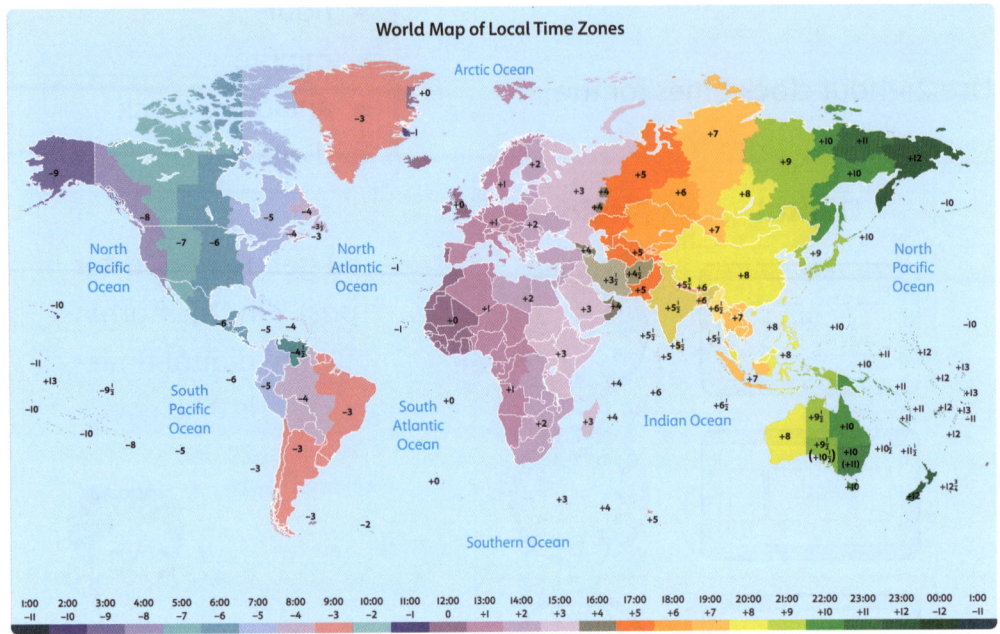

World Map of Local Time Zones

It is not the same time everywhere in the world.

3 It is 4.00 p.m. in London, United Kingdom. What time is it in each city in the table?

City	Time difference from London	Analogue time (include a.m. or p.m.)	Digital time (24-hour clock time)
Anchorage, Alaska	− 9 hours	7 a.m.	07:00
Guadalajara, Mexico	− 6 hours		
Sao Paulo, Brazil	− 3 hours		
Paris, France	+ 1 hour		
Manama, Bahrain	+ 3 hours		
Bangalore, India	+ 5.5 hours		
Osaka, Japan	+ 9 hours		
Wellington, New Zealand	+ 12 hours		

Stretch zone

Find out the time now in three different cities in the world. The cities must be on three different continents.

■ For more practice, go to Practice Book 4, page 105.

Explore

Write times

1 Draw lines to match the digital clocks with the correct analogue clocks and times in words. The first one is done for you.

Digital	Analogue	Words
1 11:05	**a**	twenty-five past 10 in the morning
2 13:40	**b**	five to 9 at night
3 12:35	**c**	twenty to 2 in the afternoon
4 09:30	**d**	five past 11 a.m.
5 18:45	**e**	twenty-five to 1 p.m.
6 10:25	**f**	half past 9 a.m.
7 20:55	**g**	quarter to 7 in the evening
8 03:50	**h**	ten to 4 in the morning

7A Different ways of telling the time

Explore (continued)

2 Complete the times on the digital and analogue clocks.

It is 3 minutes to 4 in the morning.	0 3 : 5 7	*(clock showing 3:57)*
It is twenty past 9 in the evening.	:	 *(blank clock)*
It is 27 minutes past 7 in the evening.	:	 *(blank clock)*
It is twenty-five to 10 in the morning.	:	 *(blank clock)*
It is 9 minutes to 3 in the afternoon.	:	 *(blank clock)*
It is 15 minutes past 11 at night.	:	 *(blank clock)*
It is 6 minutes past 4 in the morning.	:	 *(blank clock)*

The first one is done for you.

There are many different ways to say the time. For example, 15 minutes past 11 is also quarter past 11.

Stretch zone

Can you write the time 11:45 in five different ways?

■ For more practice, go to Practice Book 4, page 106.

7B Timetables and calendars

Discover 1

A calendar in the future

2050

January	February	March	April
S M T W T F S	S M T W T F S	S M T W T F S	S M T W T F S

January
S	M	T	W	T	F	S
						1
2	3	4	5	6	7	8
9	10	11	12	13	14	15
16	17	18	19	20	21	22
23	24	25	26	27	28	29
30	31					

February
S	M	T	W	T	F	S
		1	2	3	4	5
6	7	8	9	10	11	12
13	14	15	16	17	18	19
20	21	22	23	24	25	26
27	28					

March
S	M	T	W	T	F	S
		1	2	3	4	5
6	7	8	9	10	11	12
13	14	15	16	17	18	19
20	21	22	23	24	25	26
27	28	29	30	31		

April
S	M	T	W	T	F	S
					1	2
3	4	5	6	7	8	9
10	11	12	13	14	15	16
17	18	19	20	21	22	23
24	25	26	27	28	29	30

May
S	M	T	W	T	F	S
1	2	3	4	5	6	7
8	9	10	11	12	13	14
15	16	17	18	19	20	21
22	23	24	25	26	27	28
29	30	31				

June
S	M	T	W	T	F	S
			1	2	3	4
5	6	7	8	9	10	11
12	13	14	15	16	17	18
19	20	21	22	23	24	25
26	27	28	29	30		

July
S	M	T	W	T	F	S
					1	2
3	4	5	6	7	8	9
10	11	12	13	14	15	16
17	18	19	20	21	22	23
24	25	26	27	28	29	30
31						

August
S	M	T	W	T	F	S
	1	2	3	4	5	6
7	8	9	10	11	12	13
14	15	16	17	18	19	20
21	22	23	24	25	26	27
28	29	30	31			

September
S	M	T	W	T	F	S
				1	2	3
4	5	6	7	8	9	10
11	12	13	14	15	16	17
18	19	20	21	22	23	24
15	26	27	28	29	30	

October
S	M	T	W	T	F	S
						1
2	3	4	5	6	7	8
9	10	11	12	13	14	15
16	17	18	19	20	21	22
23	24	25	26	27	28	29
30	31					

November
S	M	T	W	T	F	S
		1	2	3	4	5
6	7	8	9	10	11	12
13	14	15	16	17	18	19
20	21	22	23	24	25	26
27	28	29	30			

December
S	M	T	W	T	F	S
				1	2	3
4	5	6	7	8	9	10
11	12	13	14	15	16	17
18	19	20	21	22	23	24
25	26	27	28	29	30	31

Key words
- week
- month
- year
- leap year
- calendar

Use this calendar for 2050 to help you answer the questions.

1 How old will you be in 2050?

2 Is 2050 a **leap year**? How do you know? _____

_____

3 What day is 26 March?   _____

4 Which months have five Wednesdays?

_____

5 Which months start on a Tuesday?

_____

6 Which month ends on a Sunday? _____

7 What day will 2051 start on? _____

Stretch zone

What day will 2060 start on? Can you explain how you worked it out?

135

■ For more practice, go to Practice Book 4, page 107.

Discover 2

School timetable

Here is Class 4's **timetable**.

	9:00 – 9:45	9:45 – 10:45	10:45 – 11:00	11:05 – 11:20	11:20 – 12:30	12:30 – 1:30	1:30 – 2:30	1:50 – 3:25
Mon	Reading and Spelling	Literacy	Break	Assembly	Maths	Lunch	PE	ICT
Tues		Literacy			Maths		Maths meeting / PHSE 1:50 – 2:30	Topic
Wed		Literacy			Maths		RE 1:50 – 2:50	Topic
Thur		Literacy			Maths		French/Music Alternate weeks	Swimming
Fri		Literacy			Maths		Topic	Topic

 Look at your own timetable. Complete the table.

How much lesson time do you have for each subject in:

- a **week**?
- a **term**?
- a **year**?

Use scrap paper or your notebook for your workings. Then write your answers clearly in the table below.

Subject	Lesson time each week	Lesson time each term	Lesson time each year

 Stretch zone

In one year, what is the difference between the number of days you are in school and the number of days you are not in school?

■ For more practice, go to Practice Book 4, page 107.

7B Timetables and calendars

Discover 3

◯ Bus timetable

Do some children at your school travel to school by bus?

Key words
- timetable
- day
- hour
- minute

| Look at the timetables for the school buses. Choose one timetable to study more closely. | ← | **Yes** | **No** | → | Ask your teacher to give you a timetable for a school bus journey. |

Talk about the timetable in pairs or groups.

The bus starts at …

The journey takes …

What time does the bus …?

Where …?

How long …?

I With a partner, write three questions about the bus timetable.

a _____
_____

b _____
_____

c _____
_____
_____

> You must be able to answer your own questions so you can check the answers!

2 Swap your questions with another pair. Check their answers.

◉ Stretch zone ➤

With a partner, write a two-step word problem about the bus timetable for another pair to solve.

■ For more practice, go to Practice Book 4, page 107.

Explore 1

Calendar problems

Luis wants to swim in the Olympics when he is older. This is a page from Luis's calendar.

Key words
- calendar
- day
- week
- date

- Use this calendar page to answer the questions.

Sunday	Monday	Tuesday	Wednesday	Thursday	Friday	Saturday
		1	2	3	4	5
6	7 Swimming club 06:15	8 School trip 08:35	9	10	11	12 Visit my cousins
13	14 Swimming club 06:15	15	16 School theatre visit 19:30	17	18	19
20	21 Swimming club 06:15	22	23	24 Last day of term	25	26 Cinema visit 18:25
27	28 Swimming club 06:15	29	30			

Work with a partner.

Swimming club lasts 1 hour 15 minutes. School starts at 08:20.

1 How many minutes are there between the end of swimming club and the start of school?

2 How many hours does Luis swim this month?

3 Luis goes to school on Mondays to Fridays. How many days is Luis at school this month?

4 School starts at 08:20 and finishes at 15:40. How many hours is Luis at school this month?

5 How many days does Luis have to wait between the theatre visit and the cinema visit?

Does Luis have any school holidays this month?

Stretch zone

Write two problems of your own using this calendar.

■ For more practice, go to Practice Book 4, page 108.

Explore 2

Train timetable

A family is on holiday in London. They want to travel by train from London to visit Oxford.

1 Complete the train timetable.

Timetable

Train	Depart London	Arrive Oxford	Journey time
A	8.22 a.m.	9.20 a.m.	58 minutes
B		9.53 a.m.	1 hour 7 minutes
C	9.00 a.m.	10.04 a.m.	
D	9.21 a.m.		1 hour 3 minutes

Train	Depart Oxford	Arrive London	Journey time
E	5.31 p.m.	6.28 p.m.	
F		6.54 p.m.	58 minutes
G	6.07 p.m.	7.16 p.m.	
H	6.31 p.m.		48 minutes

2 Which is the quickest train to Oxford? Train ☐

3 Which is the quickest train back to London? Train ☐

4 a The family arrives at the station in London at half past 8 in the morning. How long do they have to wait for the next train? ☐

b How long does that train take to reach Oxford? ☐

Stretch zone

The family travel to Oxford on train B on Friday. They travel back to London on train H on Saturday. How long do they spend in Oxford? Write the answer in days, hours and minutes.

■ For more practice, go to Practice Book 4, page 108.

Discover

Key words
- time interval
- unit of time

Units of time

1 Work with a partner. Use a stopwatch to time one minute for each activity.

Stand up straight after each touch!

   a How many times can you touch your toes in a minute?

   b How many times can you write your name in a minute?

   c Your partner starts the stopwatch. Stand up when you think a minute has passed. How many seconds have actually passed?

How did you estimate when 1 minute had passed?

2 What can you measure using each unit of time?

   Write two examples for each unit. Two are done for you.

   a Years   _people's ages_   _____

   b Minutes   _____   _____

   c Hours   _____   _____

   d Months   _a school term_   _____

   e Seconds   _____   _____

3 What is your date of birth?

   a Exactly how many years old are you?   years

   b Exactly how many months old are you?   months

I am 10 years and 3 months old, so I am $10\frac{1}{4}$ years old or 123 months old.

Stretch zone

Exactly how many days old are you?

140

7C Measuring time intervals

Key words
- how long?
- time interval
- longest
- shortest

Explore

Doctor's appointments

Think back

Remember: there are 60 minutes in an hour, so 73 minutes is 1 hour 13 minutes.

Use the doctor's appointment list to answer these questions.

1 How long is Mr Jupiter's appointment?

_____

Tuesday's appointments	
10.00 a.m.	Mr Jupiter
10.45 a.m.	Mr Saturn
11.10 a.m.	Mr Mars
11.55 a.m.	Mr Pluto
1.45 p.m.	Miss Neptune
2.05 p.m.	Miss Mercury
2.35 p.m.	Miss Uranus
3.05 p.m.	Miss Venus

2 Mr Pluto is 20 minutes late.
   What time does he arrive?

3 Miss Venus's appointment lasts 70 minutes.
   What time does her
   appointment end?

4 Which patient has the shortest appointment?

_____

5 Mr Mars arrives 20 minutes early.
   What time does he arrive?

6 Miss Neptune arrives at 1.34 p.m.

   Is she early or late? _____

   By how much? _____

7 Mr Saturn arrives exactly on time. His journey took
   55 minutes. What time did he leave home?

You could draw a number line to work out time durations.

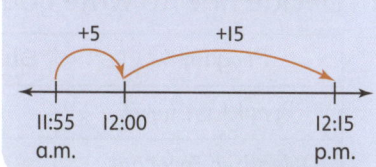

Stretch zone

Write another problem based on the appointments list. Give your problem to a partner to solve.

7 Time

141

7 Time

Connect

TV schedule

For each programme, include:

- its title
- its start and end time
- its length in minutes.

I You are going to plan a whole day's schedule for a TV channel. You must include:

- a variety of programmes, such as news, cartoons, adventure, wildlife, movies
- the start and end time for each programme
- the duration of each programme.

2 Decide how to write your schedule.

Progamme	Start and end time	Duration
Breakfast news	06:00–06:50	50 mins
Weather forecast	06:50–07:00	10 mins
Good morning world!	07:00–08:15	1 hour 15 mins
Cartoons	08:15–09:00	45 mins

You could write your schedule in a table, like I did. Or you could choose a different layout.

Stretch zone

Erase some of the durations in your schedule. Swap your schedule with a partner. Can they work out the missing durations?

Review

1 Explain why these numbers are important for learning about time.

   a I think 12 is important because _____.

   b 60 is important because there are _____.

   c 7 is the number of _____.

   d 365 is the number of _____.

   e 24 is the number of _____.

2 Write each time in words.

   a 7.45 a.m. _____.

   b 9.15 a.m. _____.

   c 7.40 p.m. _____.

3 Convert these amounts of time to minutes.

   a 120 seconds = ☐ minutes

   b $\frac{1}{2}$ hour = ☐ minutes

   c 360 seconds = ☐ minutes

4 Convert these amounts of time to days.

   3 weeks = ☐ days

   72 hours = ☐ days

   9 weeks = ☐ days

5 Convert these durations to weeks.

   $\frac{1}{2}$ year = ☐ weeks

   49 days = ☐ weeks

   2 years = ☐ weeks

Sunday	Monday	Tuesday	Wednesday	Thursday	Friday	Saturday
		1	2	3	4	5
6	7 Swimming club 06:15	8 School trip 08:35	9	10	11	12 Visit my cousins
13	14 Swimming club 06:15	15	16 School theatre visit 19:30	17	18	19
20	21 Swimming club 06:15	22	23	24 Last day of term	25	26 Cinema visit 18:25
27	28 Swimming club 06:15	29	30			

Timetable

Train	Depart London	Arrive Oxford	Journey time
A	8.22 a.m.	9.20 a.m.	58 minutes
B		9.53 a.m.	1 hour 7 minutes
C	9.00 a.m.	10.04 a.m.	
D	9.21 a.m.		1 hour 3 minutes

Train	Depart Oxford	Arrive London	Journey time
E	5.31 p.m.	6.28 p.m.	
F		6.54 p.m.	58 minutes
G	6.07 p.m.	7.16 p.m.	
H	6.31 p.m.		48 minutes

6 Tanvi's birthday is on 28 September. Enzo's birthday is on 12 December. How many days after Tanvi's birthday is Enzo's birthday?

8 Geometry – properties of shapes

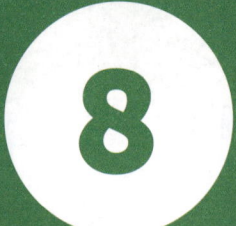

In this unit you will:

- compare and classify geometric shapes
- identify acute and obtuse angles and compare angles
- identify lines of symmetry.

How can I compare and classify the shapes I see around me?

Engage

What shapes can you see?

What are the properties of the shapes that you can see?

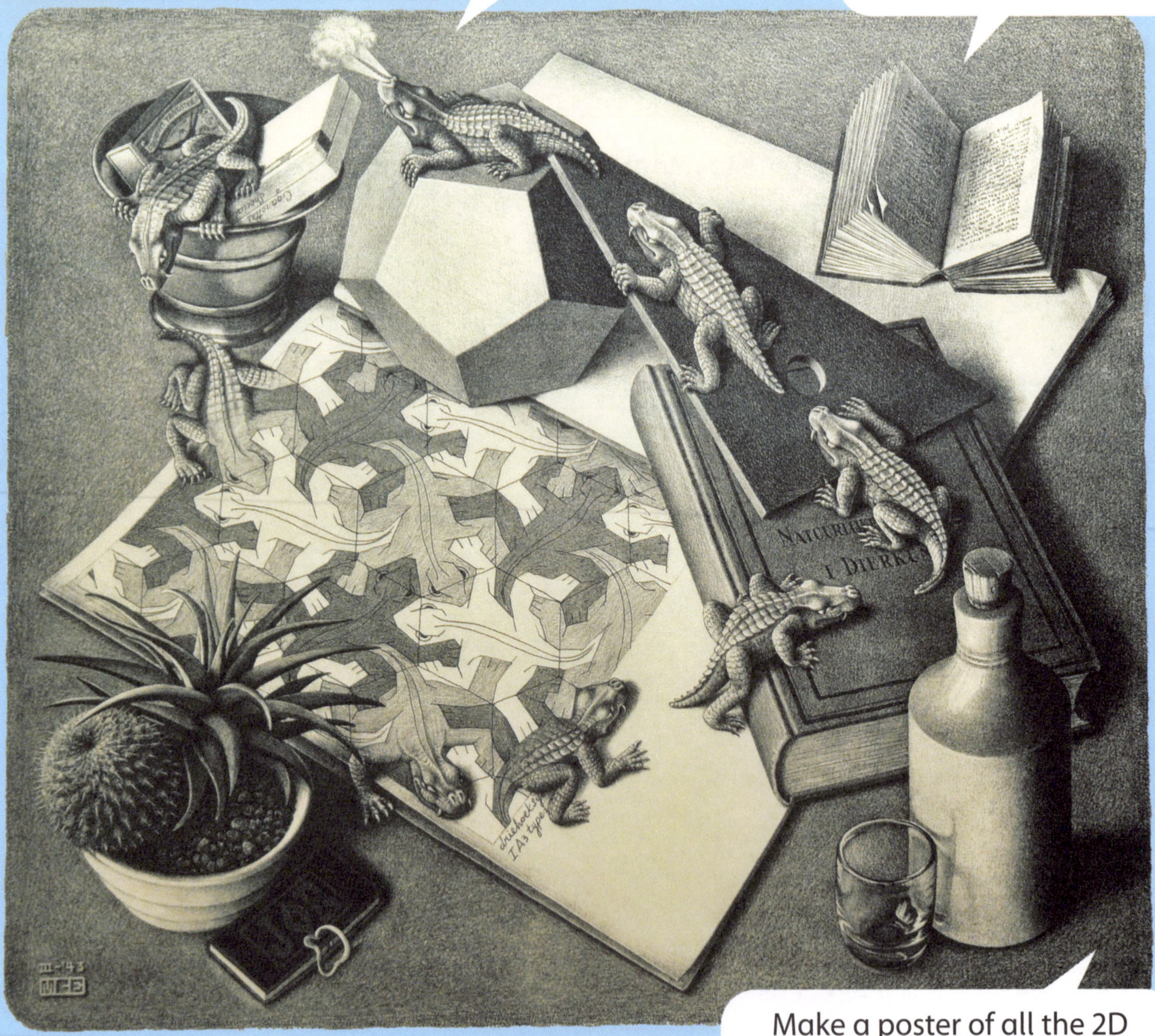

Make a poster of all the 2D and 3D shapes that you know.

Discover

Draw 2D shapes

Think back

A quadrilateral is any polygon with four sides.

Use different colours to draw these shapes. They can be regular or irregular shapes.

- a pentagon
- a hexagon
- a heptagon
- a triangle
- a quadrilateral

Use the lines on the grid to help you. You don't have to draw all the sides of your shapes on the lines.

I used the lines to help me draw an isosceles triangle.

Stretch zone

Draw three more shapes on the grid. Write the names of the shapes.

■ For more practice, go to Practice Book 4, page 112.

8A 2D shapes

Explore 1

Draw and describe triangles

Work with a partner.

Key words
- equilateral
- right-angled
- isosceles
- scalene

I   Use a ruler and a pencil to draw four different triangles in the space below.

Try to make all your triangles look as different as possible.

2   Find a partner. Look at your partner's triangles. Do any of them look like yours? What is the same and what is different?

_____

_____

3   How can you describe a triangle so that someone can draw an exact copy of your triangle?

- What information do you need to include?

_____

_____

Talk about **question 3** with your partner.

Stretch zone

Write a definition of each of these types of triangle: equilateral triangle, isosceles triangle, scalene triangle.

Classify 2D shapes

1 Look at the triangles you drew on page 146.

With your partner, decide which type of triangle each one is: equilateral, isosceles or scalene. Write E, I or S inside each triangle.

2 Draw one of each type of triangle in the space below. Label the triangles E, I and S.

Key words
• equilateral
• right-angled
• isosceles
• scalene

3 Complete the sentence to describe these shapes.

These shapes are all _____

because they all have _____ sides.

4 Look at the six shapes in **question 3**.

a Write R inside the regular shapes.

b Write O inside the **oblongs**.

c Draw a circle around the **concave** shape.

Remember: an oblong is any rectangle that is not a square.

 **Stretch zone**

Write three properties of the concave shape shown in **question 3**.

■ For more practice, go to Practice Book 4, page 114.

Key words
- property/properties
- three-dimensional (3D)
- face
- edge
- vertex/vertices

Discover

Classify 3D shapes

Work with a partner.

I Choose ten different 3D (three-dimensional) shapes.

- Decide what criteria you will use to sort your shapes using a Venn diagram.

- Label the circles in the Venn diagram below.

- Draw or write the name of each shape in the correct part of the diagram.

You might choose the properties of the faces, edges or vertices.

3D shapes

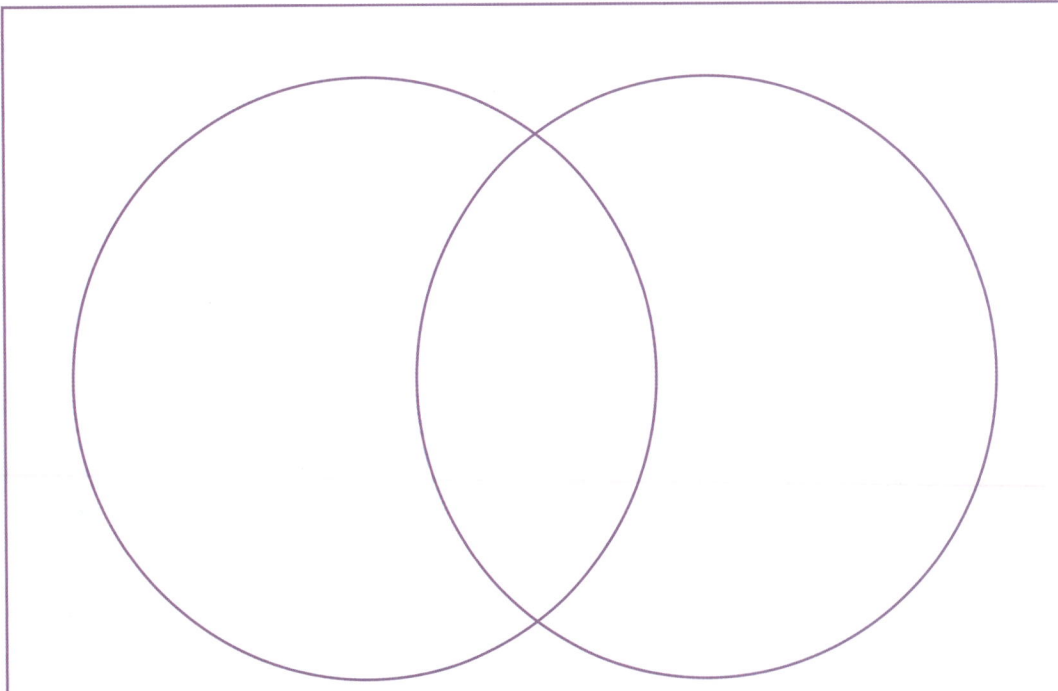

2 Are there any shapes in the intersection? _____

- What are the names of the shapes in the intersection?

_____

_____

The intersection is where the circles overlap.

 Stretch zone ➤

Can you think of a 3D shape that does not fit in your Venn diagram?

■ For more practice, go to Practice Book 4, page 115.

8B 3D shapes

Explore 1

Properties of 3D shapes

Look carefully at the 3D shapes your teacher has given you.

I   Complete this table.

	Name of shape	Number of faces	Number of vertices	Number of edges
(cone)				
(tetrahedron)				
(triangular prism)				
(cylinder)				
(hexagonal prism)				
(square-based pyramid)				
(cuboid)				
(octagonal prism)				

2   Use modelling materials or construction equipment to
make three of the shapes shown in the table.

Stretch zone

Find a 3D shape that is not in the table. Find out what it is called and
write down three properties of the shape.

■ For more practice, go to Practice Book 4, page 116.

8B 3D shapes

Explore 2

Describe the properties of 3D shapes

Key words
- property/properties
- face
- vertex/vertices
- edge

1 Describe these shapes. The first one is done for you.

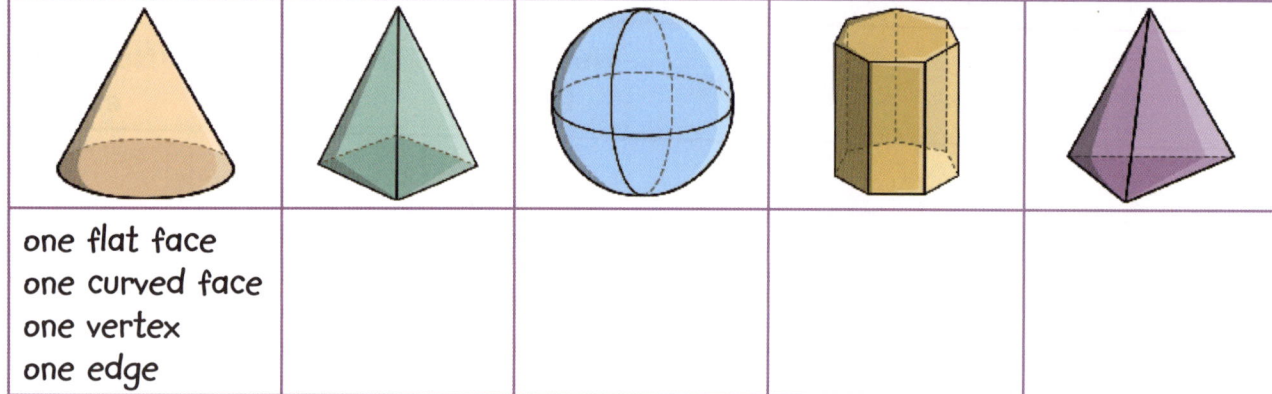

one flat face one curved face one vertex one edge				

2 Which 3D shape above matches each clue in the table below?
Think of another shape that also matches the clue.

Look carefully at some 3D shapes to help you.

What can it be?	It is a …	or a …
This shape has faces that are triangular and rectangular.		
This shape has no vertices.		
This shape has four triangular faces.		
This shape has a curved face.		
This shape has more than four rectangular faces.		

3 Write clues for two different 3D shapes. Give your clues
to a partner. Can they identify the shapes?

a _____

b _____

Stretch zone

What is the same and what is different about a prism and a pyramid?

■ For more practice, go to Practice Book 4, page 117.

Discover

Nets for a cube

You are going to draw some nets that make a cube.

Key words
- cube
- net
- face

Instructions

Remember: a cube has six square faces.

- You can arrange the six faces in many different ways, but only some of them will fold to make a cube.

- Find out which arrangements are nets of a cube.

- On the grid below, draw all the nets that you find.

Which of these two shapes is the net of a cube?

You can cut out your nets from squared paper and fold them to check if they make a cube.

 **Stretch zone**

Write some rules for drawing a net to make a cube.

8 Geometry – properties of shapes

■ For more practice, go to Practice Book 4, page 118.

8C 2D nets of 3D shapes

Explore

Key words
- net
- faces

Identify nets

I Name the shape you will make if you fold each net.

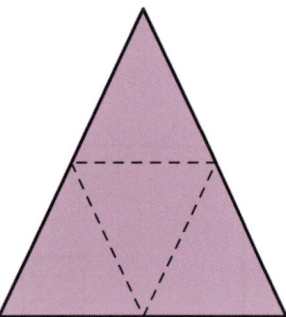

a _____

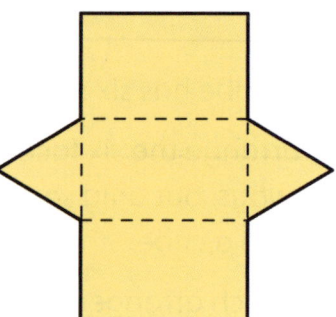

d _____

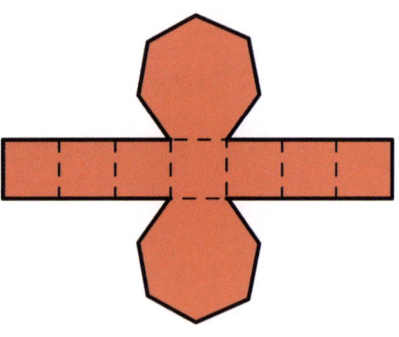

b _____

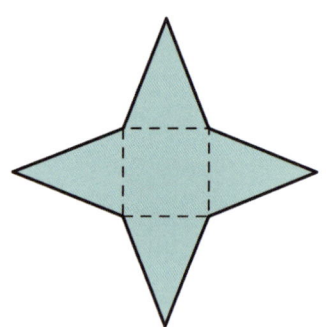

e _____

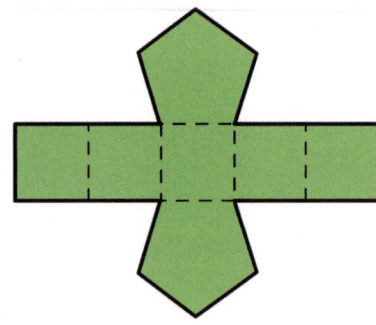

c _____

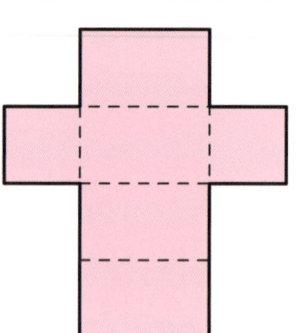

f _____

Stretch zone

Choose three of the shapes. What is the same and what is different about the nets for these shapes?

152

8D Completing symmetrical pictures

Discover

Make symmetrical patterns

1 Use counters and cubes to make your own symmetrical patterns.

   - Draw the patterns on the squared paper below.

   - You can use a horizontal, vertical or diagonal line of symmetry.

Key words
- line of symmetry
- reflective symmetry
- symmetrical

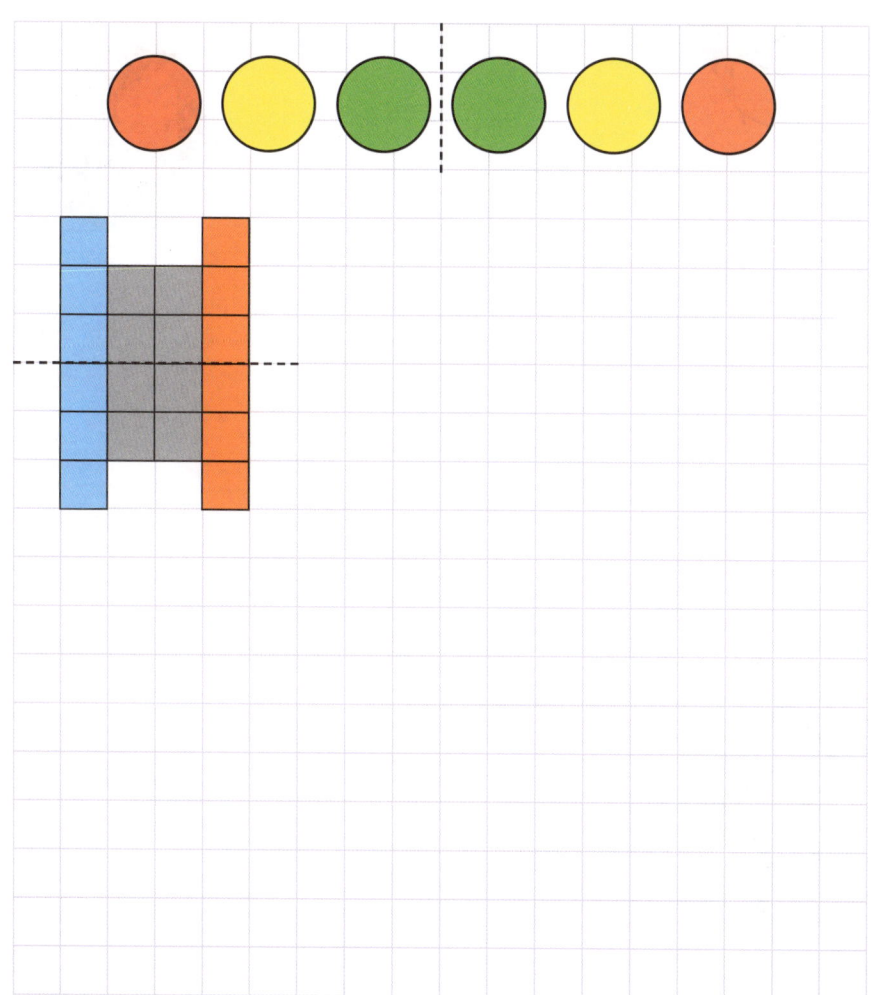

I used counters and made a symmetrical pattern with a vertical line of symmetry.

I used cubes and made a symmetrical pattern with a horizontal line of symmetry.

2 Make a symmetrical pattern using counters or cubes and ask a friend to complete it.

Stretch zone

Can you find examples of symmetrical shapes or patterns in the classroom or in your local area?

8 Geometry – properties of shapes

■ For more practice, go to Practice Book 4, page 120.

8D Completing symmetrical pictures

Explore

Complete symmetrical pictures

I Complete these symmetrical creatures.

Can you explain how you know that an image is symmetrical?

Stretch zone

Use squared paper. Draw half of a symmetrical picture for your friend to complete.

■ For more practice, go to Practice Book 4, page 121.

8E Drawing symmetrical pictures

Discover

Symmetrical cartoon characters

Key words
- line of symmetry
- mirror line

1 Design four symmetrical cartoon characters for a new computer game.

- Use at least three colours to design each character.

- Make each character quite different.

- Draw the line of symmetry for each character.

Stretch zone

Draw a character with at least two lines of symmetry.

■ For more practice, go to Practice Book 4, page 122.

Explore

Symmetrical buildings

Symmetrical buildings are pleasing to look at.

Key words
- line of symmetry
- mirror line

These buildings are symmetrical

- Design the front of an interesting symmetrical building on the squared paper below.

Stretch zone

Take a photo of a symmetrical building in your local area. Print the photo and draw the lines of symmetry on the photo.

■ For more practice, go to Practice Book 4, page 123.

Discover

Test lines of symmetry

I Look at the two lines on each shape below.

One is a line of symmetry. The other is not.

- Put a tick ✓ next to the line that is a line of symmetry.

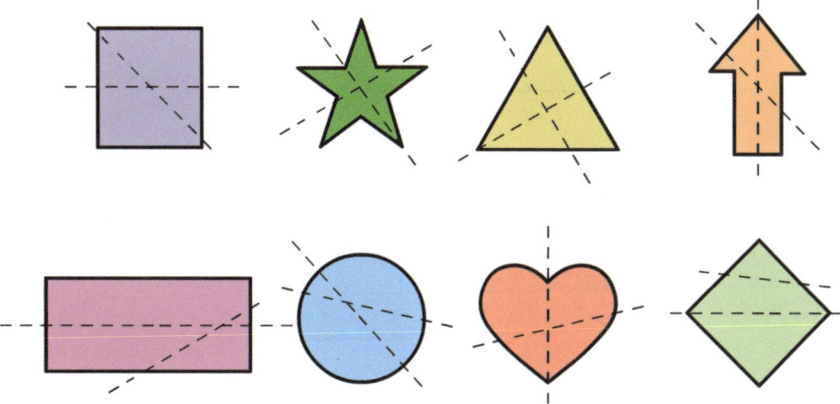

Key words
- polygon
- reflective symmetry
- line symmetry

Use a mirror to check if you are correct.

2 Draw all the lines of symmetry on these polygons to test the statement in the speech bubble.

The number of lines of symmetry in a regular polygon is equal to the number of sides of the polygon.

3 Do you agree with the statement? Explain your answer.

_____

_____

Stretch zone →

Explain how you can tell if a line is a line of symmetry.

8 Geometry – properties of shapes

■ For more practice, go to Practice Book 4, page 124.

8F Line symmetry

Explore

Key words
- polygon
- reflective symmetry
- line of symmetry

Sort 2D shapes by symmetry

1 Write the letter of each shape in the correct part of the Carroll diagram. One is done for you.

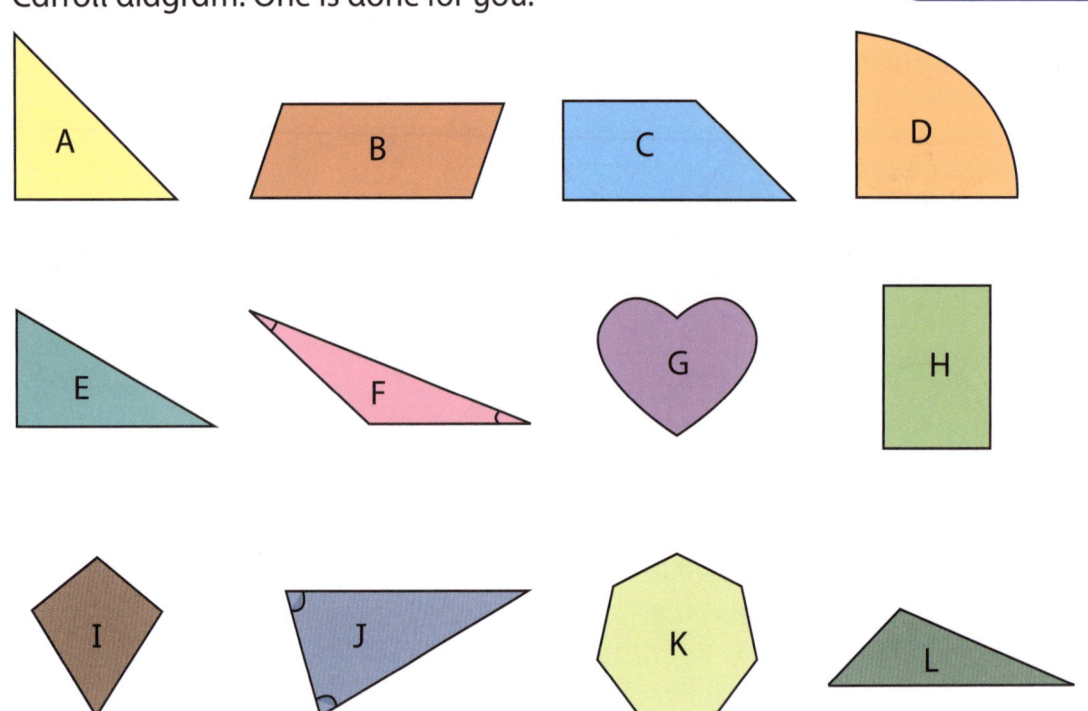

2D shapes

	At least one right angle	No right angle
At least one line of symmetry		G
No line of symmetry		

 **Stretch zone**

On all the shapes that have at least one line of symmetry, draw all the lines of symmetry. Write the name of each shape below the shape.

■ For more practice, go to Practice Book 4, page 125.

8G Angles

Discover

Make and sort angles

Think back

Remember: an angle is a measure of turn.

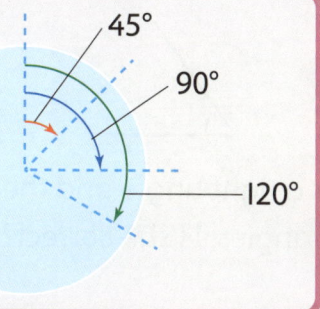

45°
90°
120°

Key words
- acute
- obtuse
- reflex
- turn

1   Make and draw eight different angles.

- Open geo-strips to make an angle.

- Carefully draw the angle on a piece of paper.

- Move the geo-strips to make a different angle.

2   Cut out your angles carefully.

- Arrange the angles in order of size.

3   Draw or stick your angles in order of increasing size.

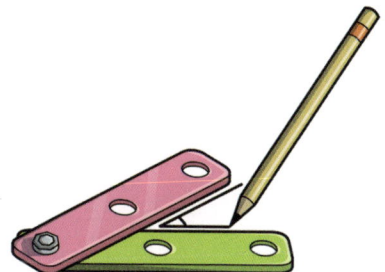

Where does a right angle fit in your order?

Stretch zone

Label your angles acute, obtuse or reflex.

■ For more practice, go to Practice Book 4, page 126.

Explore

Identify angles

I   Label these angles: right angle, acute angle, obtuse angle.

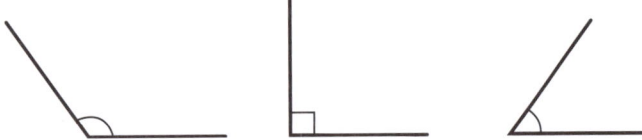

Key words
- acute
- right angle
- obtuse
- reflex

2   Rosa says that the red angle is a right angle and the other two angles are not right angles. Is she correct? Explain your answer.

What could you use to check if these angles are right angles?

3   Neema says that the purple angle is larger than the orange angle. Is she correct? Explain your answer.

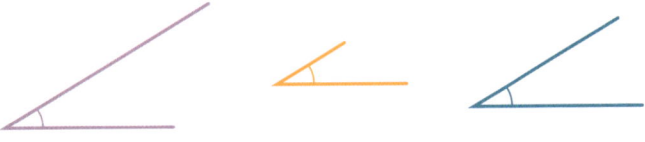

4   Find objects with an obtuse, an acute and a right angle. Draw the objects. Label the angles on your drawings.

Stretch zone

Draw an angle that is approximately 45°. Draw an angle that is approximately 135°.

■ For more practice, go to Practice Book 4, page 127.

8 Geometry – properties of shapes

Connect 1

Shape treasure hunt

In your group, walk around the school and create a shape treasure hunt.

- Make a list of ten different shapes that you see. Write their properties. Include some symmetrical shapes.

- You will need to look carefully – all around and up and down – and use your imagination.

Write ten instructions for your shape treasure hunt, for other groups to follow.

Your instructions need to clearly state:

- *where* to go
- what to *look* at
- what to *find out* or *do*.

Here are some example instructions.

- Start at the main entrance. Look at the vase on the table. What shape is it? Draw the net of the vase.
- Go to the dining hall. Look at the students' tables. What shape are they?
- Find a piece of cutlery with line symmetry. Sketch it. Draw the line of symmetry.

Light fittings may be interesting symmetrical shapes. Floor tiles may be regular polygons. Walls may have symmetrical patterns.

Try to find some unusual shapes.

Stretch zone

Swap the instructions for your treasure hunt with another group. Go on the other group's treasure hunt. Enjoy!

Connect 2

Angles in pictures

This painting is by the artist Wassily Kandinsky.

Can you see lots of angles in the painting?

1. Design your own angle picture. Include:

   - three or more right angles

   - three or more straight lines

   - three or more angles smaller than 90°

   - three or more angles greater than 90°.

2. After you have drawn your lines and angles, use colours, patterns or shapes to make your picture interesting.

You will need these things for your drawing:
colouring pens or pencils
a ruler
a protractor.

Stretch zone

Draw a different picture of angles using lines and three or more circles or parts of circles. Draw the circles using **compasses**. What interesting shapes and angles can you create with your lines?

8 Geometry – properties of shapes

Review

Use words and pictures to create a diagram of all the work you have done in this unit.
Use the suggestions below and also your own choices.
Start with the terms '2D shapes' and '3D shapes'.

prism	polygon	tetrahedron	faces
net	edges	oblong	heptagon
pyramid	regular	triangle	isosceles
symmetrical	symmetry	angle	equilateral

Here is the start of a diagram to help you.

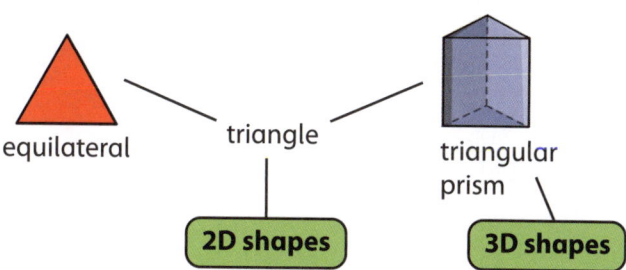

equilateral — triangle — triangular prism

2D shapes   3D shapes

In this unit you will:

- describe positions on a grid using coordinates
- describe movement using instructions such as up and down or left and right
- follow instructions to draw polygons.

? How can I describe the positions of things on a grid? How can I give instructions to draw patterns?

Engage

The teacher's desk is 4 squares to the right of the reading rug.

The whiteboard is 5 squares the left of the computer station.

The sink is 4 squares below the craft table.

Draw a map of a classroom on this coordinate grid. Follow the instructions.

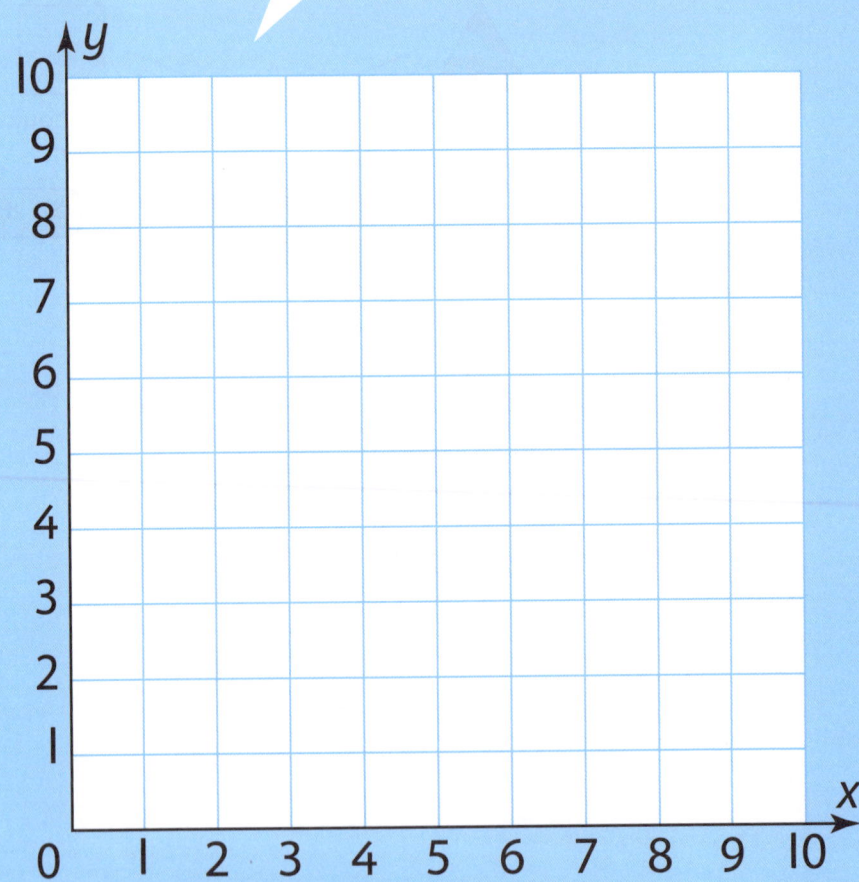

What are the coordinates of the four corners of the reading rug?

What are the coordinates of the four corners of the sink?

Draw a plan of your classroom. Use coordinates to describe the positions of objects.

Discover

Compass directions

Think back

Clockwise is the same direction as the movement of a clock's hands. Anti-clockwise is the opposite direction.

Key words

- north
- south
- east
- west
- north-east
- north-west
- south-east
- south-west

What direction are you travelling after each of the following turns?

- All turns are **clockwise**.
- The first one is done for you.

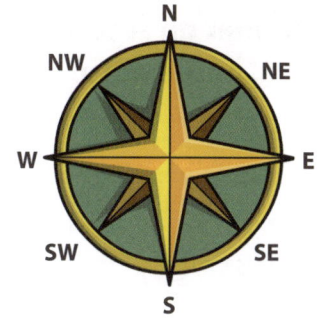

Travelling **north (N)**, turn 90°. You are now travelling _east_ .	Travelling **north**, turn 180°. You are now travelling _____.	Travelling **west (W)**, turn 90°. You are now travelling _____.	Travelling **south-east (SE)**, turn 180°. You are now travelling _____.
Travelling **north-east (NE)**, turn 90°. You are now travelling _____.	Travelling **north-west (NW)**, turn 180°. You are now travelling _____.	Travelling **south-east**, turn 90°. You are now travelling _____.	Travelling **east (E)**, turn 135°. You are now travelling _____.
Travelling **south-west (SW)**, turn 360°. You are now travelling _____.	Travelling **south (S)**, turn 135°. You are now travelling _____.	Travelling **south-east**, turn 270°. You are now travelling _____.	Travelling **north-east**, turn 135°. You are now travelling _____.

Stretch zone

On a map find places that are north, south, east and west of your school. Give a partner directions to one of the places. Can they find it?

■ For more practice, go to Practice Book 4, page 129.

9A Directions

Explore

Directions game

1 Play the directions game with a partner.

- Pick two cards from a set of digit cards 1–6.
- The tables below tell you your starting direction and the angle you need to turn.

Number on first card: starting direction	
1	NE
2	SE
3	NW
4	SW
5	E
6	W

Number on second card: angle of turn	
1	45°
2	90°
3	135°
4	180°
5	225°
6	270°

Key words
- north-east
- south-east
- south-west
- north-west

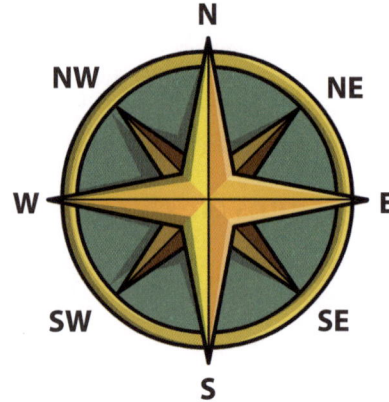

- Complete the next empty row in the table below.
- Replace your cards in the pack.

Repeat these steps until you have completed the table.

Starting direction	Angle	Final direction
E	135°	SW

All turns are clockwise.

I picked the cards 5 and 3. My starting direction is east. I turn 135° clockwise and my final direction is south-west.

2 Check the answers in your partner's table.

Stretch zone

On a map find places that are north-east, south-east, south-west and north-west of your school. Give a partner directions to one of the places. Can they find the correct place?

■ For more practice, go to Practice Book 4, page 130.

9B Giving directions to follow a path

Discover

Follow and write directions

Key words
- forwards
- clockwise
- anti-clockwise

1 Follow the instructions. Start at the red dot. Draw dots on the grid to show your path.

- Forwards 5 squares
- Turn 90° clockwise
- Forwards 5 squares
- Turn 90° clockwise
- Forwards 5 squares
- Turn 90° clockwise
- Forwards 5 squares

Start by moving up the grid.

What shape does the path make? _____

2 Write instructions to follow this path. Start at the red dot.

All turns are 90°, but do you need to turn clockwise or anti-clockwise?

_____   _____

_____   _____

_____   _____

Stretch zone

Draw a 10 × 10 grid on squared paper. Draw your own path on the grid and write the instructions to follow the path.

■ For more practice, go to Practice Book 4, page 131.

9B Giving directions to follow a path

Explore

Shop-floor directions

Key words
- clockwise
- anti-clockwise
- 90 degrees

Here is a shop floor plan.

- Yellow areas are walkways.
- Blue areas are displays and cash desks.

Exit

Entrance

1 Write instructions for a route from the Entrance to the Exit.

In each instruction, include:
- the number of squares
- a compass direction
- the direction of turn
- the angle in **degrees**.

_____

_____

_____

_____

_____

_____

_____

_____

_____

 2 Write instructions for a different route from the Entrance to the Exit.

 **Stretch zone**

Draw a different map on a grid and write instructions from one place to another. Can a partner follow your directions correctly?

■ For more practice, go to Practice Book 4, page 132.

Discover

Find the treasure

1 Play this game with a partner. You each have:

five treasure chests (T)

three lots of gold bars (G)

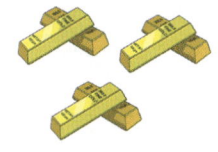

two pirates (P).

- Decide where to put your treasure, gold and pirates on your coordinate grid below. Write T, G or P.

- Do not show your partner your grid.

2 Take turns to choose coordinates on your partner's grid.

- If there is treasure or gold at that coordinate, you win it.

- If there is a pirate at that coordinate, you miss a turn.

- The winner is the first person to collect all their partner's treasure and gold.

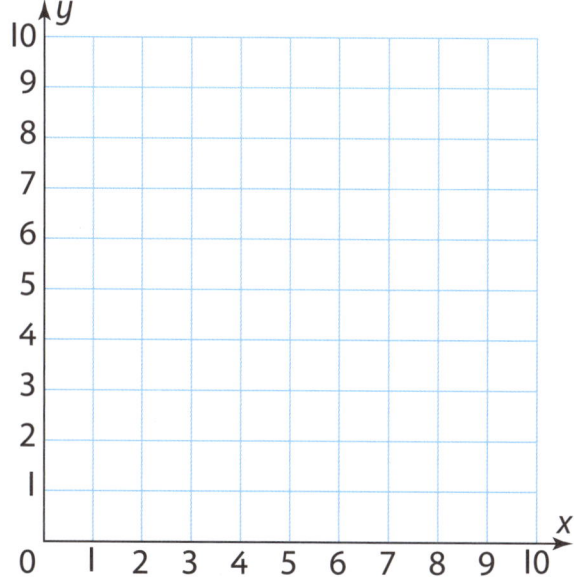

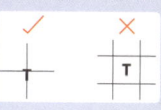

You need to write the letters where two lines intersect, not in the middle of a square.

I want to put a treasure chest at point (3,7) so I write 'T' on that point on my grid.

Remember: we write coordinates by moving across and then up, so the x-axis coordinate comes first.

 **Stretch zone**

Design your own game using coordinates. Play your game with a partner.

9 Geometry – position and direction

169

Explore

Island coordinates

Look at the map of an island.

1 Write the coordinates of each place.

a Cave (☐ , ☐)

b Harbour  (☐ , ☐)

c Flag (☐ , ☐)

d Hills (☐ , ☐)

e Castle (☐ , ☐)

f Lookout (☐ , ☐)

g Pond (☐ , ☐)

2 Draw on the map:

a two more hills at (3,5) and (5,9)

b two more flags at (3,1) and (1,7).

3 Add two more places to the map. Write the coordinates.

Picture of place	Name of place	Coordinates

Stretch zone

Rafael says 'The order of the coordinates in a coordinate pair does not matter.' Is he correct? How do you know?

■ For more practice, go to Practice Book 4, page 134.

9D Translations

Discover

Translate shapes

Translation means sliding a shape to a new position on a grid. The shape stays the same size and does not turn.

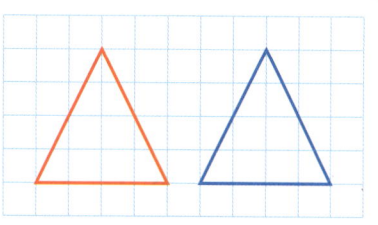

Key words
- translation
- slide
- up/down
- left/right

I slid the red triangle five squares to the right to the position of the blue triangle.
I wrote:
Translation: **right** *5 squares*

Draw a simple shape on each grid. Slide it and describe the move as a translation. Draw two translations that slide left or right. Draw two translations that slide up or down.

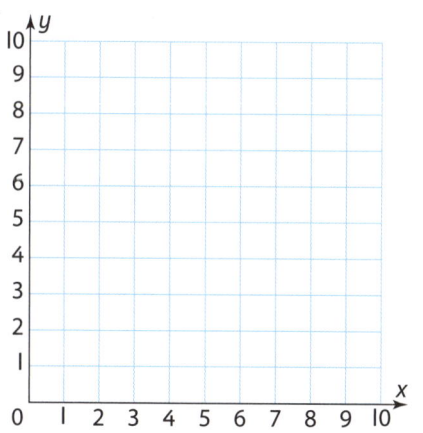

Translation: _____

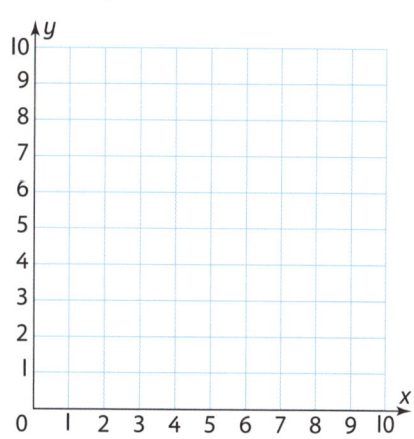

Translation: _____

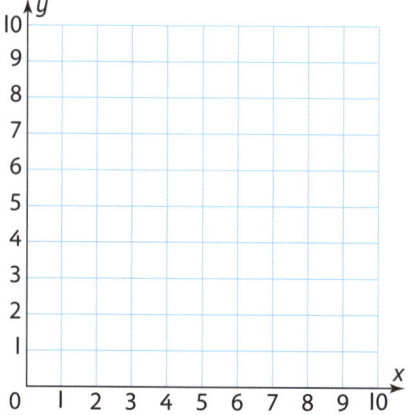

Translation: _____

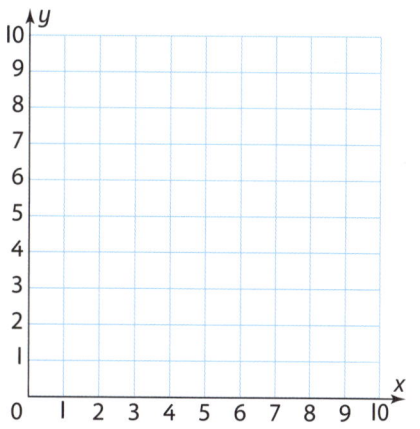

Translation: _____

 **Stretch zone**

Draw a two-step translation that slides left or right and then up or down.

■ For more practice, go to Practice Book 4, page 135.

9D Translations

Plot translated shapes

Remember: in a translation, the shape does not turn or reflect. It just slides in one or more directions on the grid.

Key words
- translation
- up/down
- left/right

- Draw each shape on each grid after the translation.

1 Left 1 square

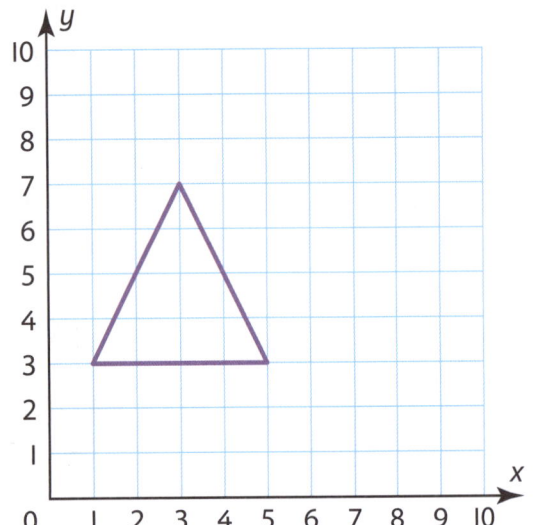

2 Up 2 squares, right 2 squares

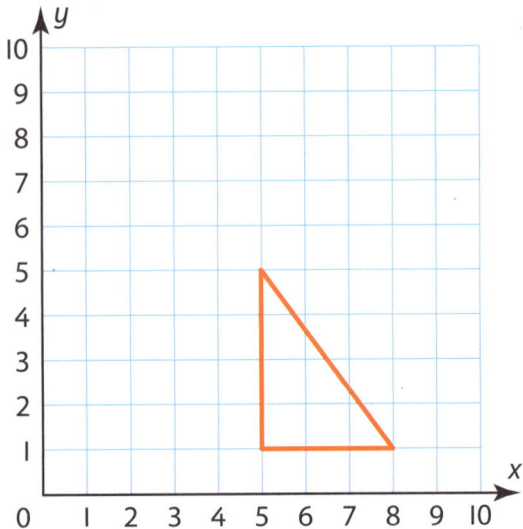

3 Down 2 squares, right 1 square

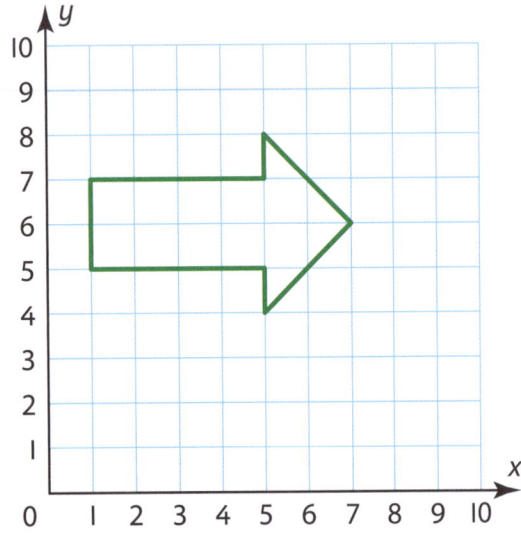

4 Left 4 squares, down 3 squares

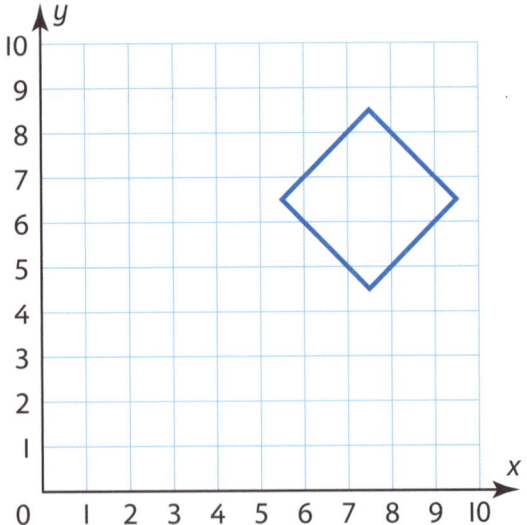

Stretch zone°

What changes and what stays the same in the coordinates after each type of translation: up, down, left and right?

172

■ For more practice, go to Practice Book 4, page 136.

Discover

Plot shapes on a grid

Draw the following shapes on these grids and write the coordinates of the vertices.

1

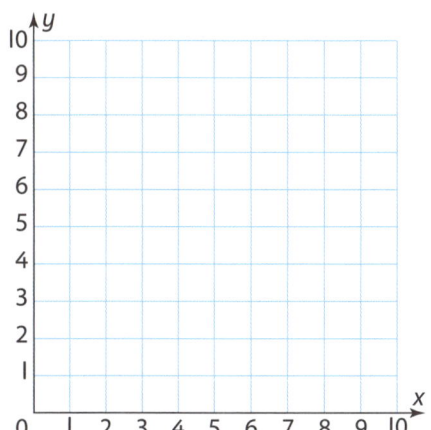

Square: side length 3

Coordinates of vertices:

_____

2

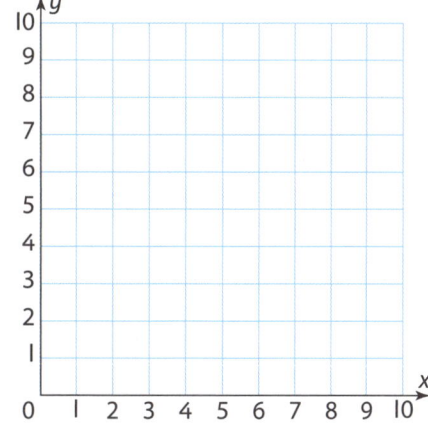

Rectangle: width 3, length 5

Coordinates of vertices:

_____

You can choose anywhere on the grid to draw each shape.

3

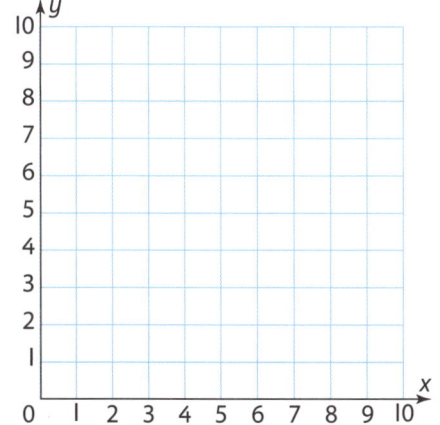

Right-angled triangle: height 4

Coordinates of vertices:

_____

4

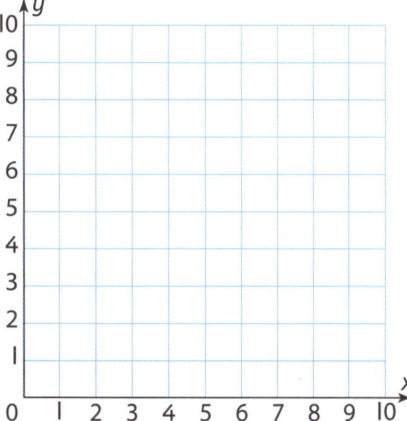

Your own choice of shape

Coordinates of vertices:

_____

Stretch zone

Look at the coordinates for the square. Can you describe the pattern in the coordinates? Can you explain why this pattern occurs?

■ For more practice, go to Practice Book 4, page 137.

Explore

What is the shape?

Remember: to plot each point, first move along the x-axis and then up the y-axis.

- Plot the coordinates on each grid. What shape do you make?

1

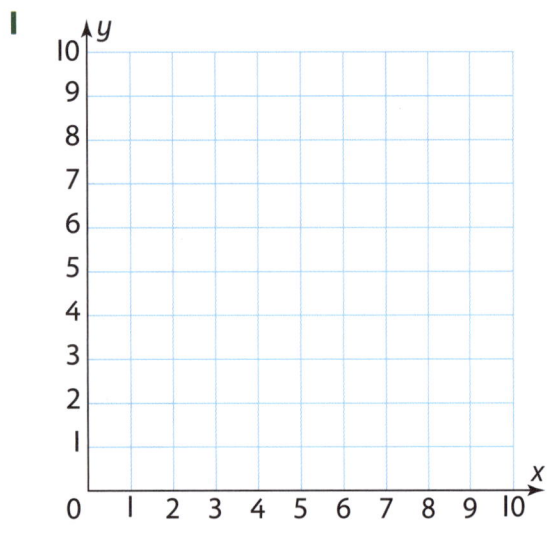

(1,1) (7,1) (1,4) _____

2

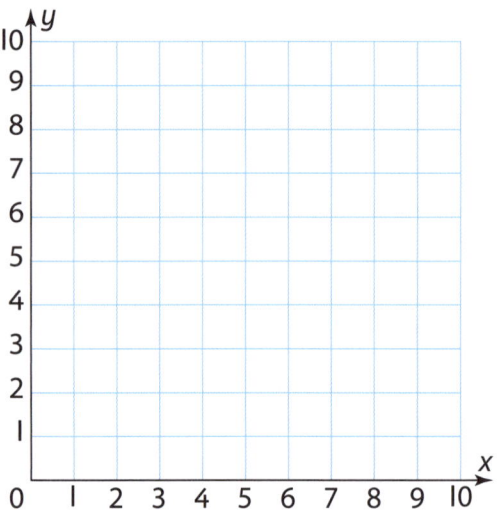

(2,2) (2,7) (7,7) (7,2) _____

3

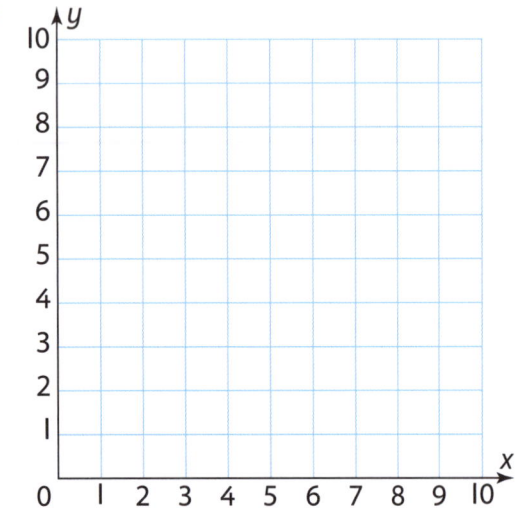

(4,1) (1,4) (6,9) (9,6) _____

4

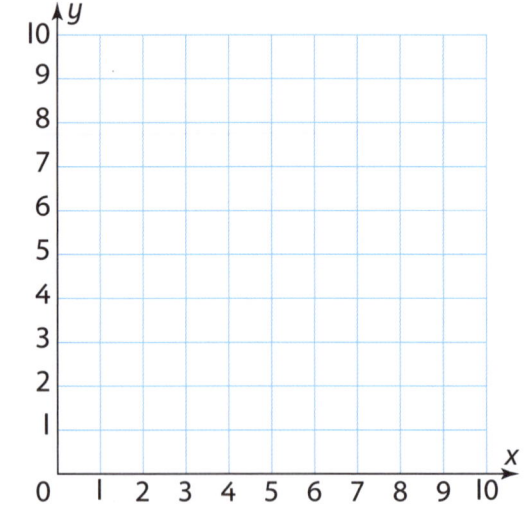

(3,2) (2,4) (5,7) (8,4) (7,2) _____

Stretch zone

Did you guess what the shapes would be before you drew them, just by looking at the coordinates? Explain your answer.

■ For more practice, go to Practice Book 4, page 138.

I can describe the positions of things using coordinates. I can describe how things move using translations.

Connect

Translation patterns

These patterns all use translations. They are made by translating a shape or a pattern of shapes over and over again.

You are going to draw your own translation pattern.

1 First, plan your pattern on a coordinate grid.

- Draw a pattern in the centre of your grid.

- Translate the pattern up, down, left and right, and draw it again.

2 When you are happy with your pattern, draw it on a larger piece of paper.

- Repeat your pattern many times to fill the paper.

Stretch zone

Create a classroom display of all your translation patterns.
Below your translation pattern, write the translation that you used on the coordinate grid.

9 Geometry – position and direction

1 Write the correct direction letters on the points of this compass.

2 On the coordinate grid below draw a shape that has vertices at these coordinates: (1,5) (3,7) (5,5) (3,3).

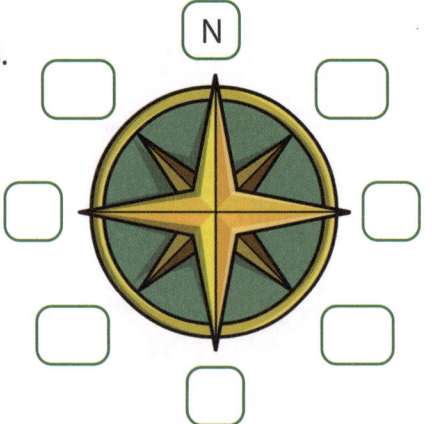

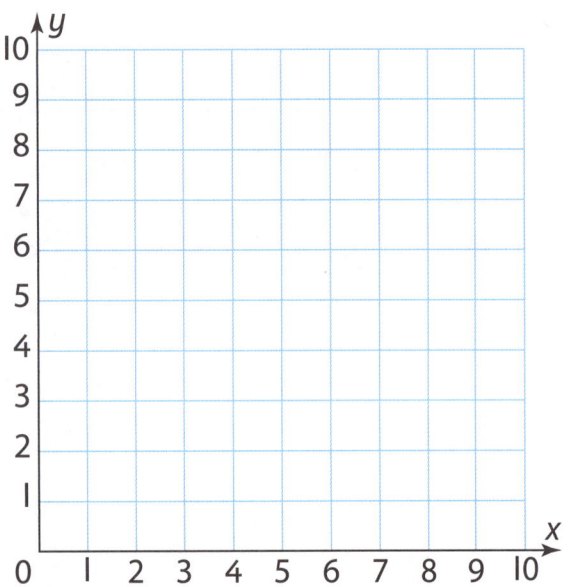

3 Translate the shape from **question 2** right 4 squares. Draw the new shape on the grid.

4 Draw a dot at point (1,6) and another dot at point (8,9). Describe the translation of the dot in two different ways.

a _____

b _____

5 Gabriel draws a rectangle on this grid and writes the coordinates of points
A (1,7), B (5,7) and C (1,4).
He then translates the rectangle.

a What are the coordinates of point D?

(⬜ , ⬜)

b Describe Gabriel's translation.

_____

_____

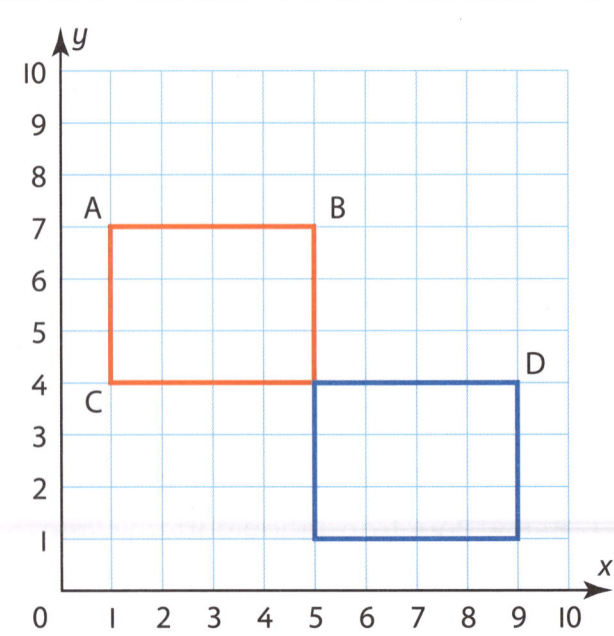

?

What are some different ways to collect, organise and present **data**? What can data tell us?

In this unit you will:

- interpret and present data using bar charts and time graphs
- solve problems using data presented in bar charts, pictograms, tables and other graphs.

Engage

What might the bars in this chart represent?

What might the scale be?

What is this sort of chart called?

What is missing from this chart?

What graphs and charts do you see in the media?

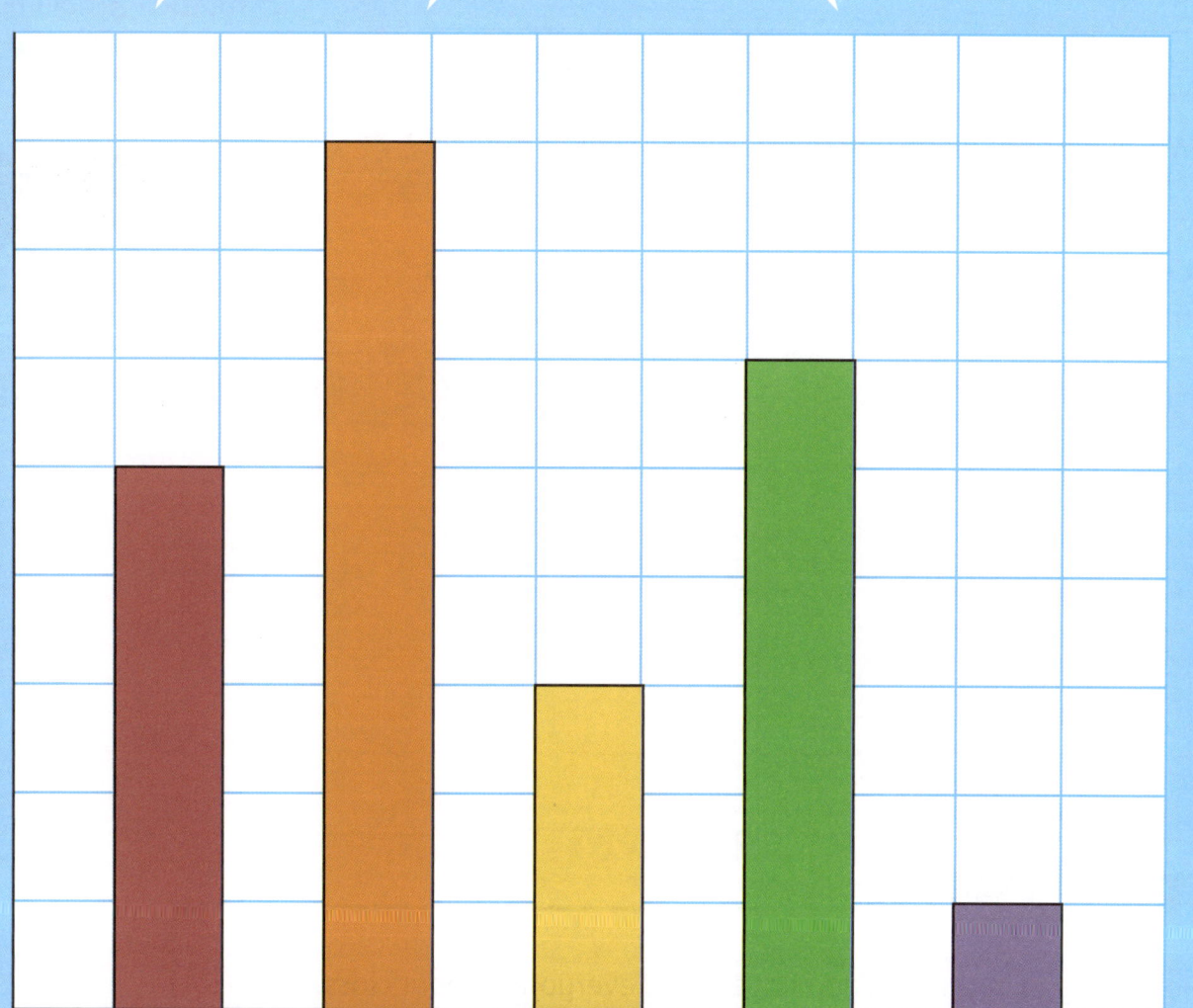

10A Collecting, presenting and interpreting data

Discover 1

Collect data

1 Choose **one** of these questions to investigate.

   a Which place would you most like to visit for a day?

   b Which place would you most like to visit for a school trip?

   c Which country in the world would you most like to visit?

   Our group chose question _____.

2 Choose five popular destinations as the answer options for your question.

   _____   _____

   _____   _____

   _____

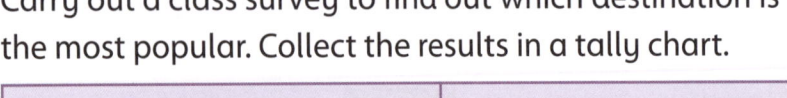

Our group chose question **a**. We wrote: a safari park, the seaside, a museum, a football stadium, a shopping centre.

3 Which destination do you think will be the most popular?

   _____

4 Carry out a class survey to find out which destination is the most popular. Collect the results in a tally chart.

Destination	Tally	Frequency

Stretch zone

How can you check that you have asked everyone in your class?

■ For more practice, go to Practice Book 4, page 140.

Discover 2

Present data

Key words
- most popular
- least popular
- bar chart
- pictogram

1. Look at the data that you collected in your tally chart on page 178. Choose a type of chart to present the data. You can choose a bar chart or a pictogram.

2. Draw your chart here.

 3. Write a short report about the information that your chart shows. Answer these questions?

- Which was the most popular choice and which was the runner-up?

- Was your prediction correct?

- Look at your chart on this page and the table on page 178. Which shows the information more clearly?

The runner-up means the second most popular.

Stretch zone

What is the same and what is different about each way of presenting the data?

10 Statistics

179

Explore 1

Ice-cream data

The tally chart below shows the number of different flavours of ice-cream sold at an ice-cream shop in one day.

1 Complete the 'Frequency' column.

Flavour	Tally	Frequency
Vanilla	ɪɪɪɪ ɪɪɪɪ ɪɪɪɪ ɪɪɪɪ ɪɪɪɪ ɪɪ	
Chocolate	ɪɪɪɪ ɪɪɪɪ ɪɪɪɪ ɪɪɪɪ ɪɪɪ	
Strawberry	ɪɪɪɪ ɪɪɪɪ ɪɪɪɪ ɪ	
Mango	ɪɪɪɪ ɪɪ	
Coconut	ɪɪɪɪ ɪɪɪɪ ɪɪɪɪ ɪɪɪɪ	

2 Draw a bar chart to present this data.

Label the axes clearly and give your chart a title.

3 Write three facts that the bar chart shows.

_____

_____

_____

Stretch zone

Carry out a survey about favourite ice-cream flavours. Draw a bar chart to show the results. How does your bar chart compare to the bar chart above?

■ For more practice, go to Practice Book 4, page 142.

Explore 2

Class survey data

The students in Class 4 had a day's holiday. They collected data about where everyone went on their day's holiday.

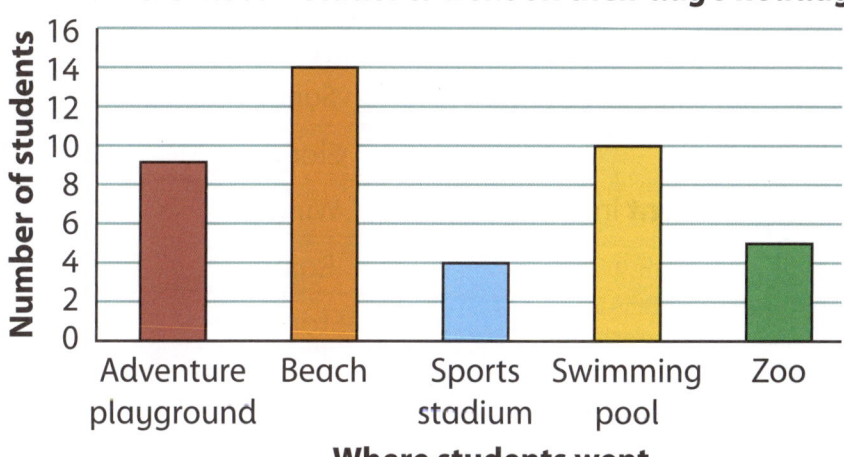

Where Class 4 students went on their day's holiday

1 Tick ✓ the statements that you agree with.

   a Ten students went to the swimming pool.

   b More students went to the adventure playground than to the zoo.

   c Two more students went to the zoo than to the sports stadium.

   d The beach was the most popular destination.

   e It is summer.

   f The sports stadium was a popular choice.

   g More than half the students went to the swimming pool.

   h There are 40 students in Class 4.

2 For each statement that you have not ticked, explain to a partner why you disagree.

Are there any statements that you cannot agree or disagree with?

Stretch zone

Write two more true statements about the data shown in the bar chart.

10 Statistics

181

■ For more practice, go to Practice Book 4, page 143.

Discover 1

Different scales

The table shows some weather data from a country in Europe collected over three months.

You are going to investigate the effect of using different **scales** in bar charts.

Key words
- scale
- interval
- bar chart

Weather	Number of days
Sunny	35
Cloudy	21
Windy	9
Rainy	19
Stormy	7

1 Decide with your group what scale you will each use for the vertical axis.

- Make sure that each person uses **different** intervals on their scale.

2 Draw your bar chart.

Give the bar chart a title and label the axes and scales clearly.

3 Compare the effects of the different scales in your group. Which scale do you think shows the data most clearly? Why?

_____

_____

Stretch zone

Would you always choose the same scale for a similar weather chart? Can you explain your answer?

■ For more practice, go to Practice Book 4, page 144.

Discover 2

Interpret scales

Look at the bar chart you drew on page 182.

Key words
- scales
- intervals
- bar chart

1 Work together as a group to make up six questions about the data shown in the bar chart.

a _____

b _____

c _____

d _____

e _____

f _____

2 Look at these two bar charts. Explain why they might mislead people.

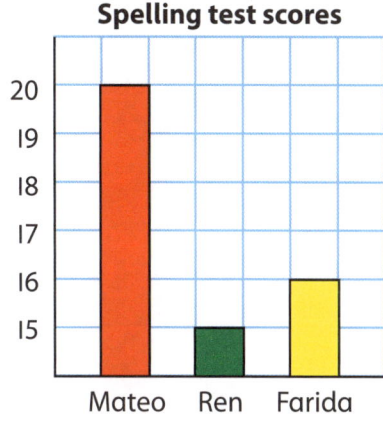

Spelling test scores

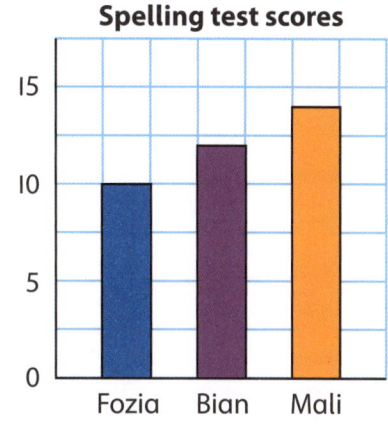

Spelling test scores

Swap books with another group and answer their questions.

Look carefully at the scales on the y-axis of the two charts.

_____

_____

_____

Stretch zone

On squared paper, draw one bar chart to show all the spelling test scores from **question 2**. Choose a better scale for your chart.

10 Statistics

183

Explore 1

Research and collect data

> We can collect some data by counting, for example, the number of people who visit a museum on each day of the week. This sort of data is called **discrete** data.
>
> Sometimes, we cannot count data; we must measure it because it keeps changing. For example, temperature, length or mass. This sort of data is called **continuous** data.

Key words
- temperature
- above and below freezing
- positive
- negative

The table below shows the average hottest and coldest temperatures in December in some countries around the world. This is continuous data, because it is always changing.

Use the internet to complete the table. Then choose three more countries and add the data.

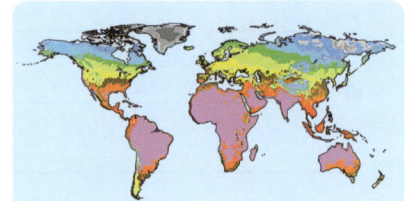

Country	December average highest temperature (°C)	December average lowest temperature (°C)
Greenland (North Pole)	⁻26	⁻31
USA (Alaska, Anchorage)	⁻5	⁻12
Australia (Sydney)	25	17
New Zealand (Wellington)	17	12
United Kingdom (London)	9	5
Russia (Siberia)		
Finland (Tampere)		
Spain (Madrid)		
Saudi Arabia (Jeddah)		
United Arab Emirates (Dubai)		
South Africa (Johannesburg)		

Stretch zone

Use books or the internet to find three more examples of continuous data and three examples of discrete data.

■ For more practice, go to Practice Book 4, page 146.

Interpret temperature data

I Use the data for the first five countries in the table on page 184. Choose a scale for the thermometer and label the scale. Mark the high and low temperatures for all five countries.

Key words

- temperature
- above and below freezing
- positive
- negative

2 Use your thermometer to answer these questions.

a Which country has the highest temperature? _____

b Which country has the lowest temperature? _____

c What is the difference in temperature between the highest and lowest temperatures in Alaska? _____

d Which country has the biggest difference between the highest and lowest temperatures? _____

e Which country has the smallest difference between the highest and lowest temperatures? _____

 **Stretch zone**

Using this data, write an easy problem and a more difficult problem. Give your problems to a partner to solve.

10 Statistics

185

■ For more practice, go to Practice Book 4, page 147.

Explore 3

Interpret tables

Work with a partner.

Key words
- frequency table
- data
- scale
- interval

 This frequency table shows the number of people who visited a museum each day in one week.

Monday	Tuesday	Wednesday	Thursday	Friday	Saturday	Sunday
15	35	83	90	42	51	64

1 On squared paper, draw one bar chart each to present this data. You will each use a different scale.

- Bar chart 1: use one square to represent 5 people.

- Bar chart 2: use one square to represent 10 people.

Discuss your bar chart with your partner before you draw it.

Remember to add the title and to label the axes.

2 Now answer these questions.

a Which bar chart was easier to draw? Why?

_____

b Which bar chart was easier to read? Why?

_____

c Which is the most popular day at the museum? Why do you think this is?

_____

d Which is the least popular day? Why do you think this is?

_____

Stretch zone

Make up two questions about the museum data that involve calculations. Give your questions to another pair to solve.

■ For more practice, go to Practice Book 4, page 147.

10C Time graphs

■ For more practice, go to Practice Book 4, page 148.

Discover

Water temperature over time

Time graphs often show continuous data. They show how measurements such as height or temperature change over time. We can use a line graph to show change over time.

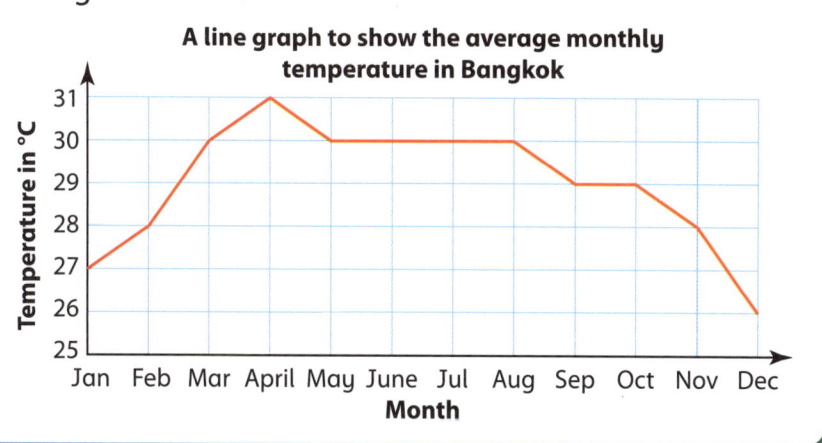

A line graph to show the average monthly temperature in Bangkok

Key words
- continuous data
- line graph
- time graph

💬 Work in a group.

1 Fill a container with water and measure the temperature of the water.

- Place the container outside.

- Take the temperature of the water every 30 minutes for 2 hours.

2 Complete this table.

Time (in minutes)	0	30	60	90	120
Temperature (in °C)					

3 On squared paper, draw a time graph to present the data in the table.

> Can you tell a partner what sort of data your water temperature data is: discrete or continuous? Can you explain why?

Stretch zone

Use your time graph to estimate the water temperature at 45 minutes, 75 minutes and 105 minutes. Explain your thinking.

Explore

Draw time graphs

Mia measured the height of her plant every two weeks. This table shows the measurements.

Time (in weeks)	Week 1	Week 3	Week 5	Week 7	Week 9
Height (in cm)	2	4	7	11	17

This table shows a baby's mass each month in the first 6 months of its life.

Time (in months)	Month 1	Month 2	Month 3	Month 4	Month 5	Month 6
Mass (in kg)	3	3.5	4	4.5	5	7

Work with a partner. Draw one time graph each:

- Time graph 1: the height of Mia's plant

- Time graph 2: the baby's mass.

Discuss your time graph with your partner before you draw it.

Line graphs are often used for time graphs.

What do you notice about how a baby grows over time?

Stretch zone

Use your time graph to estimate the height of Mia's plant in Week 2 and in Week 6. Explain your thinking.

188

10D Using Venn diagrams and Carroll diagrams

Discover 1

Use Venn diagrams

Key words
- Venn diagram
- criterion/criteria
- intersection
- union

1 Choose two cards from a set of digit cards 1–8 and make the two different 2-digit numbers.

- Write the numbers in the Venn diagram.

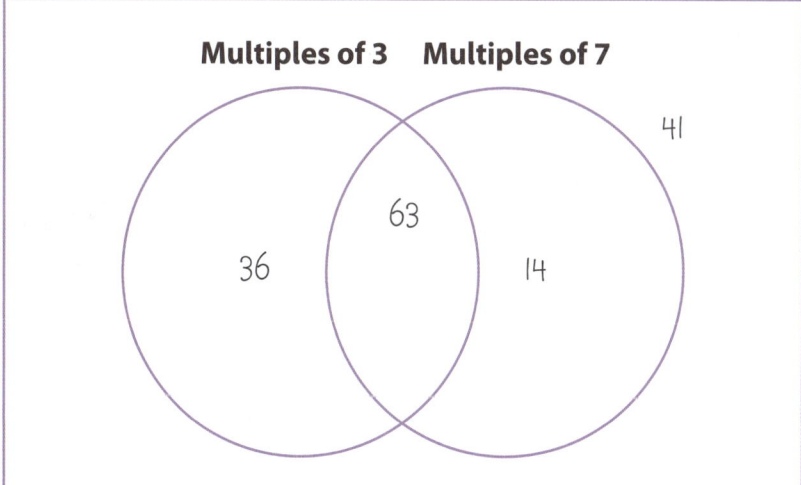

I chose 6 and 3
I made 36 and 63

Then I chose 1 and 4
I made 14 and 41

- Continue until you start to get repeat numbers.

2 How many 2-digit numbers go in the intersection?

3 In this Venn diagram, write five names of students.

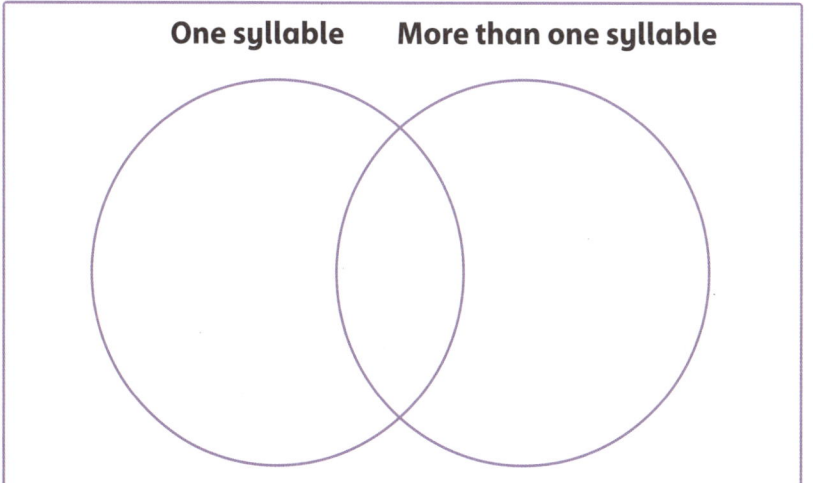

Can there be any names in the intersection? Why?

Stretch zone

Draw your own Venn diagram. Choose the sorting criteria. Write three items in each circle, three in the intersection and three outside the circles.

10 Statistics

■ For more practice, go to Practice Book 4, page 150.

Discover 2

Use Carroll diagrams

Key words
- Carroll diagram
- criterion/criteria

Think back

On page 189 you used a Venn diagram to sort names. A Carroll diagram is a better way to sort names according to the number of syllables.

Try to find at least one name for each section of the diagram.

1 Label this Carroll diagram to answer these questions.
- Does the first name have more than one syllable?
- Does the family name have more than one syllable?

2 Write ten names of students in your class in the correct sections of the Carroll diagram.

3 Are there any students in your class whose names have only one syllable in both their first name and family name? Where do these names go in the diagram?

Use the diagram to answer the question.

 Stretch zone

Are there any students in your class whose names do not fit in the diagram? Explain your answer.

■ For more practice, go to Practice Book 4, page 150.

Explore 1

Sort using a Venn diagram

Some students sorted these shapes into a Venn diagram.

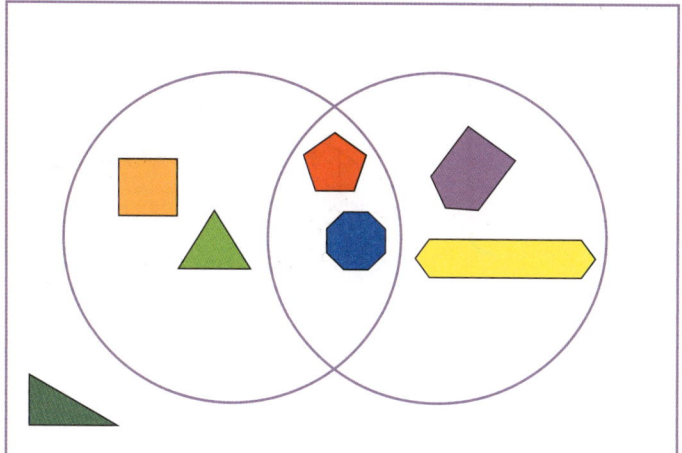

Key words
- Venn diagram
- criterion/criteria
- intersection
- union

I What do you think the sorting criteria were?

_____

2 Label the Venn diagram below with the sorting criteria.

3 Write the names of the shapes in this Venn diagram.

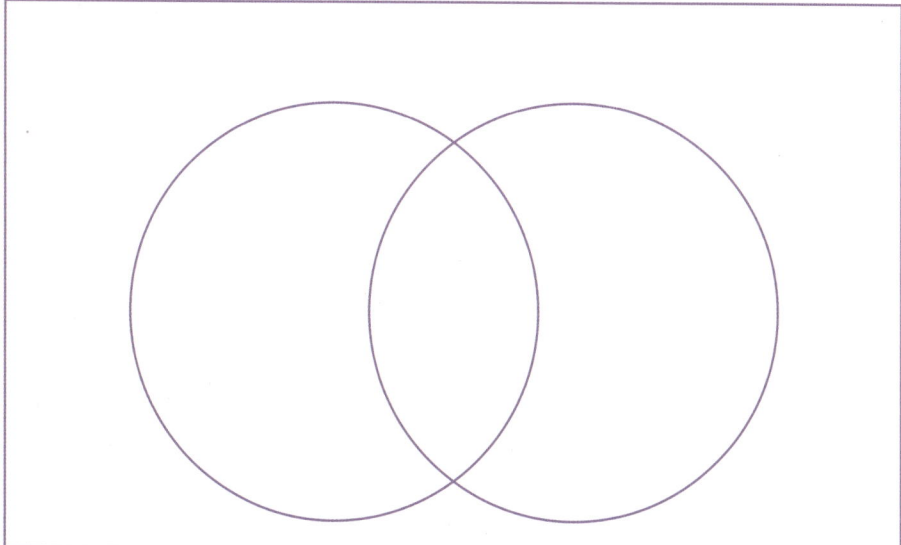

4 Add the names of five more shapes to the Venn diagram.

Stretch zone

Name three shapes that do not fit in either circle.

■ For more practice, go to Practice Book 4, page 151.

10D Using Venn diagrams and Carroll diagrams

Explore 2

Sort using a Carroll diagram

Key words
- Carroll diagram
- criterion/criteria

1   Use the Carroll diagram to sort the words in this rhyme.

> Incy wincy spider climbed up the water spout,
>
> Down came the rain and washed the spider out,
>
> Out came the sun and dried up all the rain,
>
> So incy wincy spider climbed up the spout again.

- Remember: the vowels are a, e, i, o, u.

	Only one vowel in the word	Not only one vowel in the word
Word begins or ends with a vowel		
Word does not begin or end with a vowel		

2   Make up a Carroll diagram to sort numbers.

- Choose your own sorting criteria.

Try to find at least three numbers to put in each section.

Stretch zone

Create a Carroll diagram to sort shapes. Choose your own criteria.

■ For more practice, go to Practice Book 4, page 151.

10 Statistics

Connect

○ What is your favourite?

Work in a group. You are going to find out about your class's favourite things in a range of different categories.

1 Choose one category to investigate. Here are some ideas.

- Favourite lesson
- Favourite fruit
- Favourite sport
- Favourite TV programme
- Favourite game
- An idea of your own ...

2 Write a sensible question for your **survey**.

_____

3 Choose five or six answer options.

4 Predict two things that you think you will find out.

_____

_____

5 Carry out the survey with everyone in your class.

6 Complete this tally chart. Write each total in the frequency column.

Options	Tally	Frequency

 7 On squared paper, draw a bar chart of your results.

8 Were your predictions correct?

_____

Take time to make your bar chart as accurate as possible.

 Stretch zone

Write one thing you found out that surprised you. How can you extend your investigation?

10 Statistics

Review

You are the teacher!

A group of students have carried out a survey to find out how many people used the facilities at a leisure centre in one day.

They collected this data.

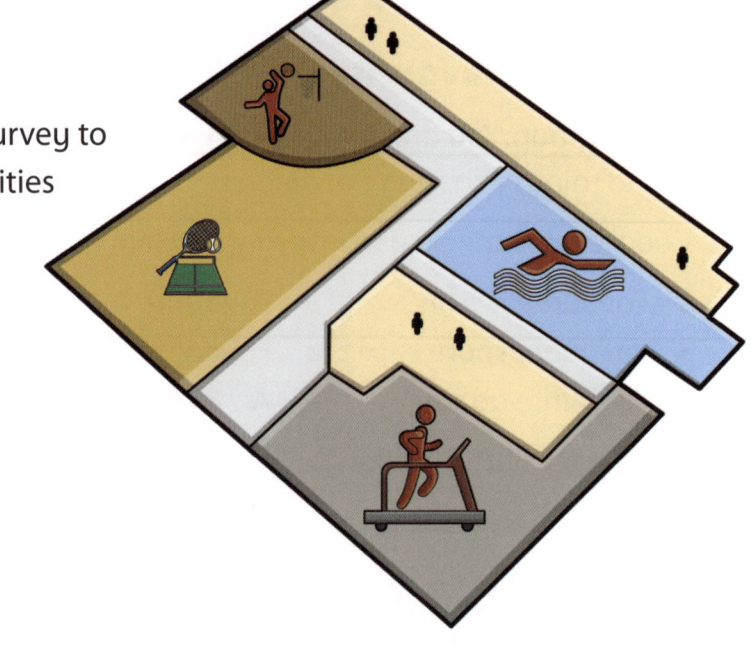

> Number of people who used each facility:
>
> Swimming pool: 45
>
> Basketball court: 40
>
> Tennis court: 32
>
> Gym: 61

The students want to present their data so it is easy to understand.

1 Write step-by-step instructions for the students to:

- present their data in a frequency table
- draw a bar chart to show their data.

2 Swap your instructions with a partner. Follow each other's instructions to create a frequency table and draw a bar chart.

3 Discuss the table and chart with your partner. Were the instructions accurate? Was anything missing?

4 Write two questions about the data shown in your bar chart.

_____

_____

_____

_____

- Give your questions to a partner to answer.

These students have never created a frequency table or drawn a bar chart before, so include every detail!

You must follow the instructions exactly.

Glossary

acute

_____

_____

_____

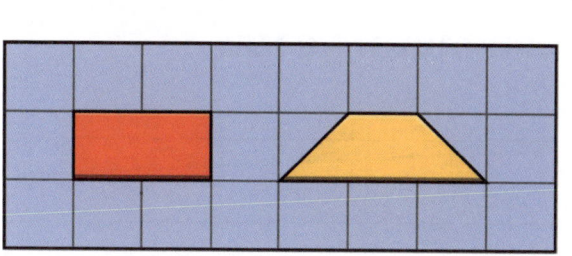

acute angle

right angle

area

_____

_____

_____

The **area** of both these shapes is 2 cm²

associative law

_____

_____

_____

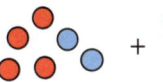 +  =

(5 + 2) + 3 = 10

5 + 5 = 10

base

_____

_____

_____

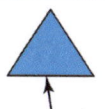

base of triangle

base of cone

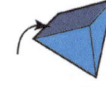

square-**based** pyramid

column addition and subtraction

_____

_____

_____

```
   1 7 9          8 ⁴5̶ ¹0
 + 1 8 2        - 1 3 5
 ─────────      ─────────
   3 6 1          7 1 5
   1 1
```

A **column addition**   A **column subtraction**

commutative law

_____

_____

_____

5   +   2   =   7

2   +   5   =   7

consecutive

_____

_____

_____

14, 15, 16, 17 are **consecutive** numbers

7, 9, 11, 13 are **consecutive** odd numbers

⁻5, ⁻4, ⁻3, ⁻2 are **consecutive** negative numbers

continuous data

_____

_____

_____

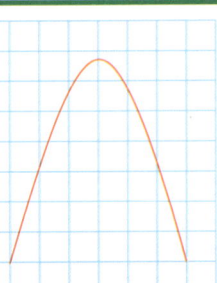

A line graph shows **continuous data**

coordinates

_____

_____

_____

The **coordinates** of A are (1,3)
The **coordinates** of B are (3,2)

data

_____

_____

_____

A computer stores lots of
items of **data**

decimal fraction

_____

_____

_____

A **decimal fraction**
uses a decimal point:

$0.5 = \frac{5}{10} = \frac{1}{2}$

$0.25 = \frac{25}{100} = \frac{1}{4}$

decimal number

_____

_____

_____

3.27

This **decimal number** is made up of:
3 ones, 2 tenths, 7 hundredths

decimal place

3.5 has 1 **decimal place**

12.56 has 2 **decimal places**

0.228 has 3 **decimal places**

3.234677 written to 2 **decimal places** is 3.23

decimal point

42.6

decimal point

This number is forty-two **point** six

degree

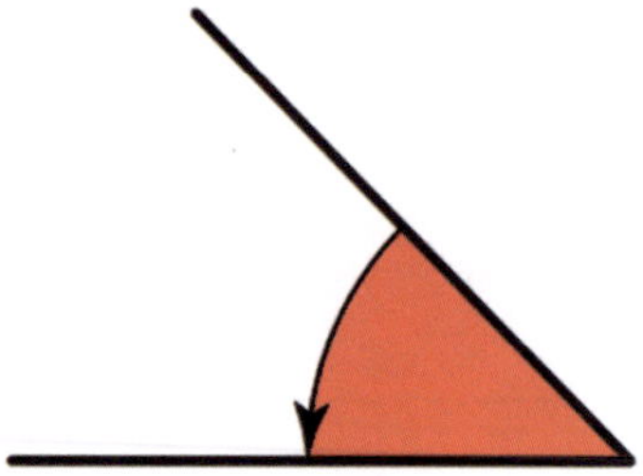

This angle measures 45 **degrees**
We write this as 45°

discrete data

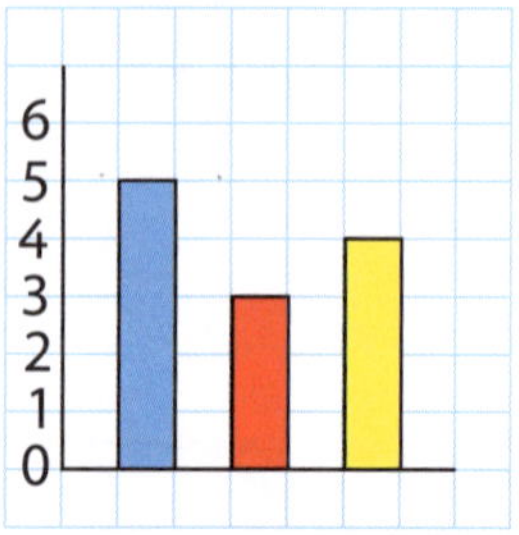

The bar chart show **discrete data**

distributive law

_____

_____

_____

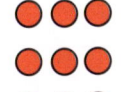

$3 \times (3 + 2)$ $\qquad$ $3 \times 3 \ + \ 3 \times 2$

equilateral triangle

_____

_____

_____

Equilateral triangles

equivalent

_____

_____

_____

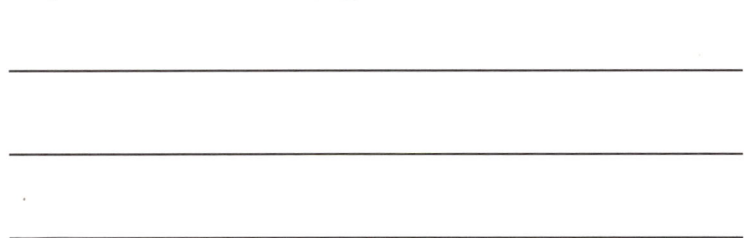

Equivalent fractions:

$$\frac{4}{6} = \frac{2}{3} \qquad \frac{3}{4} = \frac{75}{100}$$

Simplifying makes an **equivalent** fraction: $\quad \dfrac{10^2}{15^3} = \dfrac{2}{3}$

factor

_____

_____

_____

3 is a **factor** of 21

7 is a **factor** of 63

2 and 7 are both **factors** of 14

greater than (>)

_____

_____

_____

12 > 7

12 is **greater than** 7

heptagon

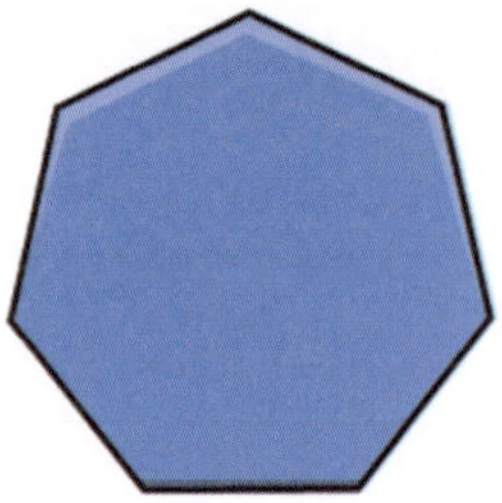

_____

_____

_____

A regular
heptagon

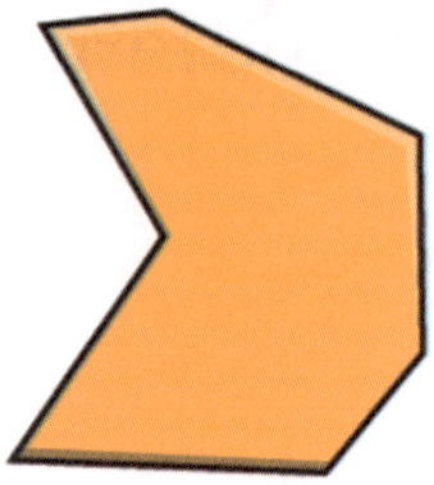

An irregular
heptagon

hundredths

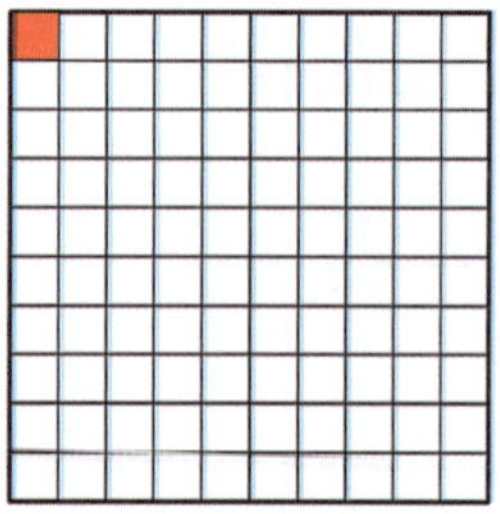

_____

_____

_____

One **hundredth** of the
square is coloured red

integer

_____

_____

_____

−4 −3 −2 −1 0 1 2 3 4

negative
integers

positive
integers

inverse

_____

_____

_____

The **inverse** of + 7 is – 7

17 + 7 = 24

24 – 7 = 17

The **inverse** of × 4 is ÷ 4

12 × 4 = 48

48 ÷ 4 = 12

irregular

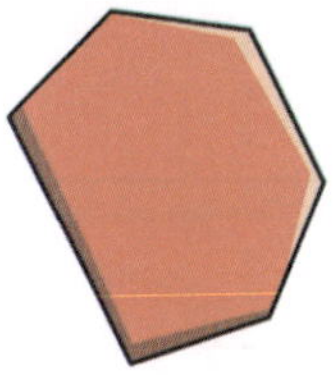

_____

_____

_____

An **irregular** heptagon

An **irregular** triangle

isosceles triangle

_____

_____

_____

isosceles triangles

less than (<)

_____

_____

_____

15 < 20

15 is **less than** 20

mass

_____

_____

_____

An astronaut's **mass** is the same on the Earth as on the Moon. But an astronaut weighs less on the Moon than on Earth.

metric unit

_____

_____

_____

Length	Mass	Capacity
millimetre	gram	millilitre
centimetre	kilogram	centilitre
metre	tonne	litre
kilometre		

These are all **metric units**

millennium

_____

_____

_____

I **millennium** = 10 centuries

millimetre

_____

_____

_____

1000 **millimetres** = I metre

10 **mm** = I cm

multiple

_____

_____

_____

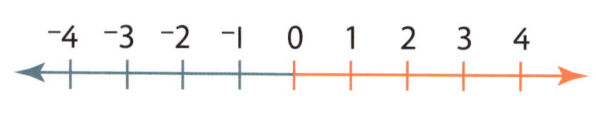

The **multiples** of 10 are circled

negative number

_____

_____

_____

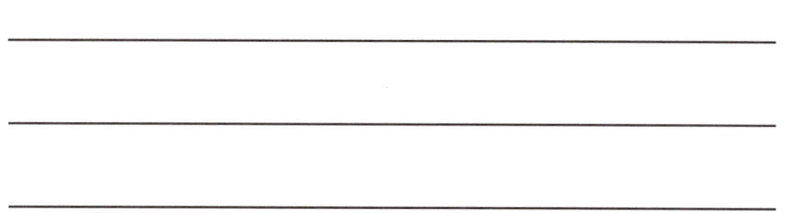

You can write negative 2 as ⁻2 or −2.

oblong

_____

_____

_____

 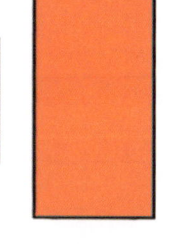

oblongs

obtuse

_____

_____

_____

Obtuse angles are greater than a right angle

perimeter

_____

_____

_____

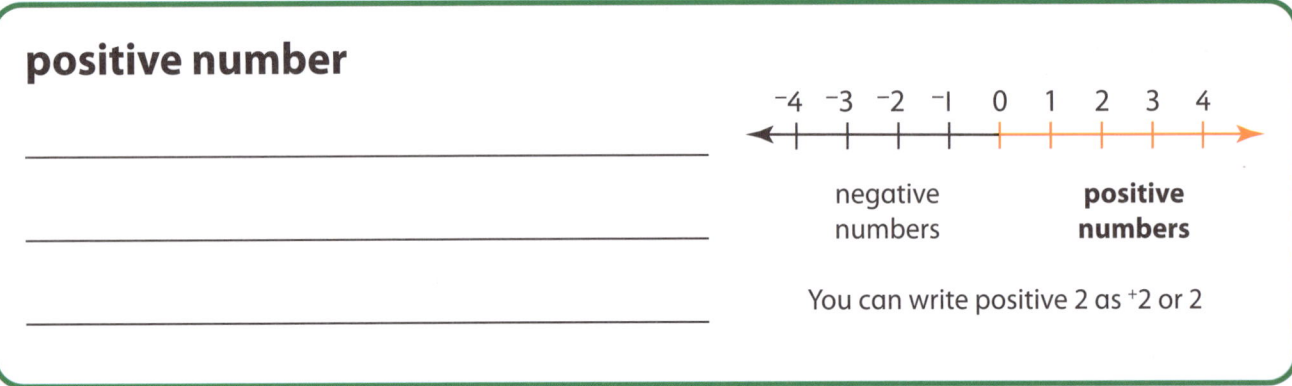

the **perimeter** of a rectangle

the **perimeter** of a triangle

positive number

_____

_____

_____

−4 −3 −2 −1 0 1 2 3 4

negative numbers

positive numbers

You can write positive 2 as $^+2$ or 2

property (*plural:* properties)

_____

_____

_____

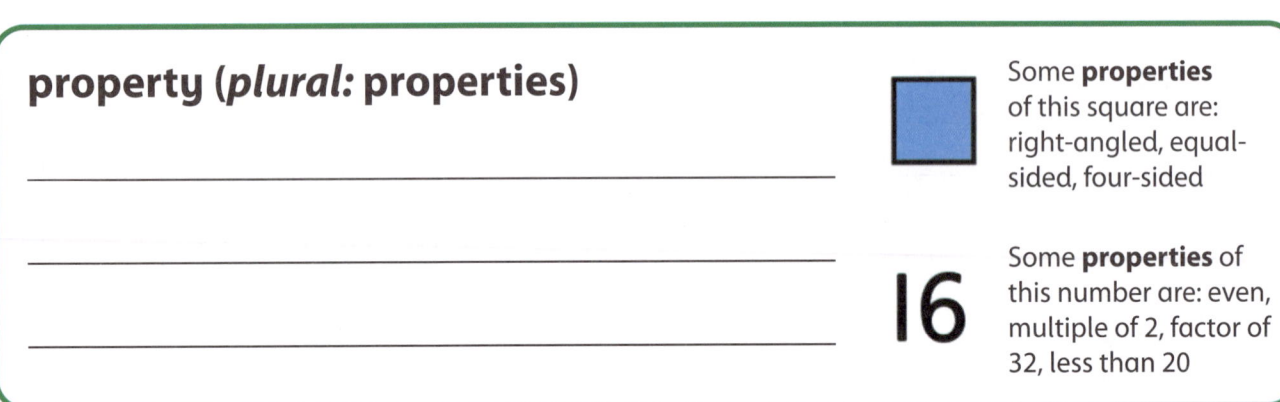

Some **properties** of this square are: right-angled, equal-sided, four-sided

16

Some **properties** of this number are: even, multiple of 2, factor of 32, less than 20

quadrilateral

_____

_____

_____

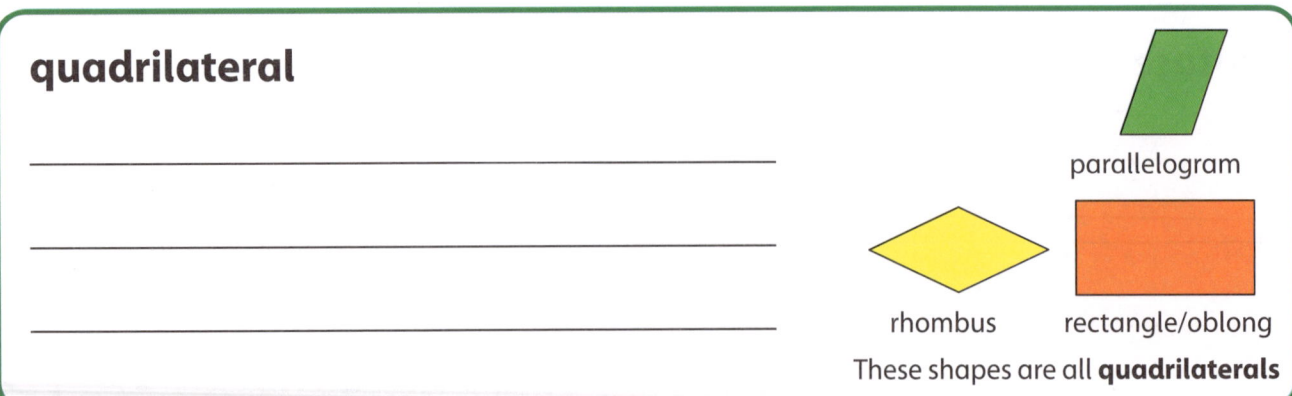

parallelogram

rhombus

rectangle/oblong

These shapes are all **quadrilaterals**

rectilinear

_____

_____

_____

rectilinear shapes

reflect

_____

_____

_____

reflection

object

mirror

Reflecting is like flipping
a shape over

regular

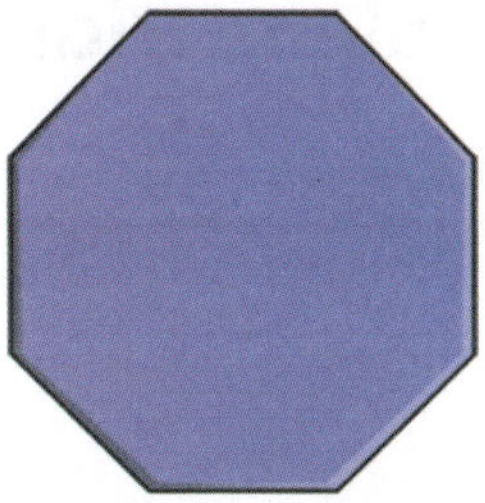

_____

_____

_____

A **regular** octagon

right angle

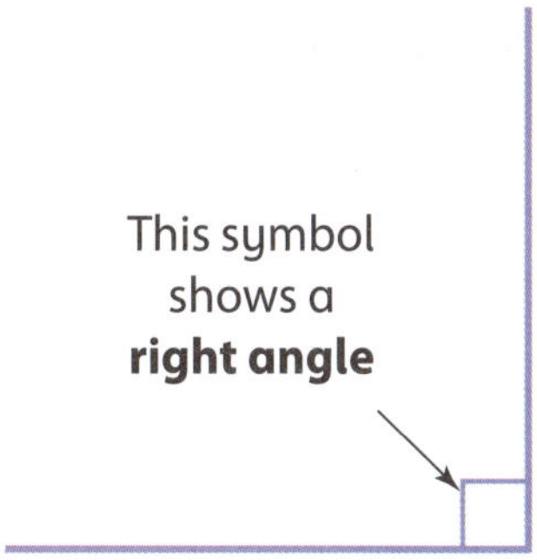

_____

_____

_____

This symbol
shows a
right angle

Roman numerals

_____

_____

_____

rotate

_____

_____

_____

The circle is **rotating**

scalene triangle

_____

_____

_____

A **scalene triangle** can be acute or obtuse

simplify

_____

_____

_____

$$\frac{10}{40} = \frac{5}{20} = \frac{1}{4}$$

We **simplify** fractions by dividing the denominator and numerator by the same number

square centimetre

_____

_____

_____

A I cm square has an area of
I **square centimetre** (I cm²)

survey

_____

_____

_____

symmetry / line of symmetry

_____

_____

_____

The kite has **line symmetry**

three-dimensional (3D)

_____

_____

_____

Three-dimensional shapes

time graph

_____

_____

_____

This **time graph** shows the average monthly temperature in Bangkok

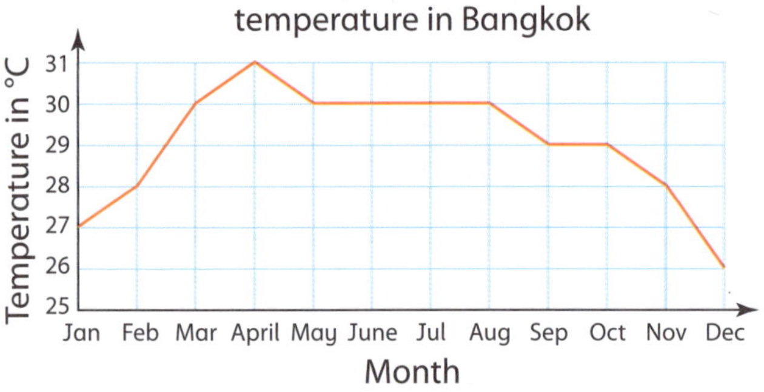

translation

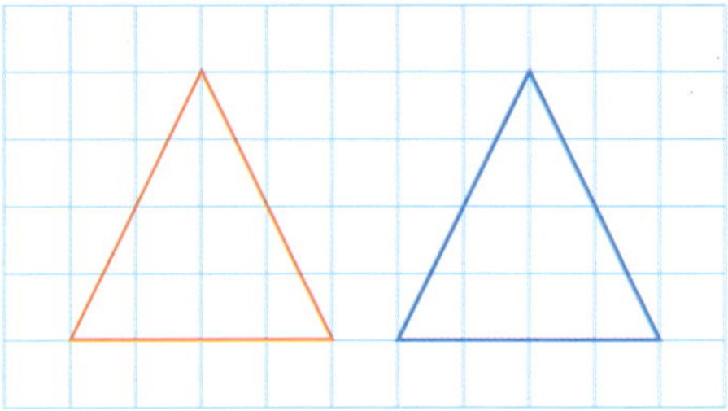

_____

_____

_____

The red triangle has been **translated** 5 squares to the right

two-dimensional (2D)

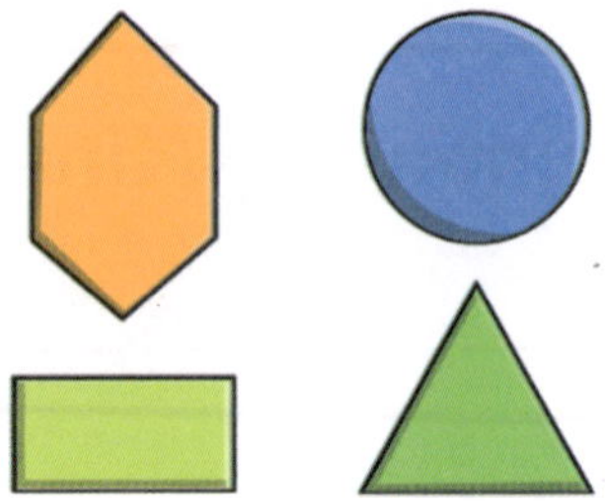

_____

_____

_____

Two-dimensional shapes

unit fraction / non-unit fraction

_____

_____

_____

These are **unit fractions**:

$\dfrac{1}{2}$ $\dfrac{1}{5}$ ← The numerator is 1

These are **non-unit fractions**:

$\dfrac{2}{3}$ $\dfrac{4}{5}$ ← The numerator is not 1